Including and Supporting Learners of English as an Additional Language

Also available from Continuum

Bilinguality and Literacy 2nd edition, Manjula Datta and Colin Baker

English Language Teacher's Handbook, Joanna Baker and Heather Westrup

Language Acquisition and Development, Brian Tomlinson

Perspectives on Participation and Inclusion, Suanne Gibson and Joanna Haynes

Including and Supporting Learners of English as an Additional Language

Madeleine Graf

continuum

Continuum International Publishing Group
The Tower Building   80 Maiden Lane,
11 York Road   Suite 704
London SE1 7NX   New York, NY 10038

www.continuumbooks.com

British Library Cataloguing-in-Publication Data
A catalogue record for this book is available from the British Library.

ISBN: 978-1-4411-6267-0 (paperback)
       978-1-4411-8139-8 (hardcover)

Library of Congress Cataloging-in-Publication Data
Graf, Madeleine.
Including and supporting learners of English as an additional language/
Madeleine Graf.
   p. cm.
Includes bibliographical references.
ISBN 978-1-4411-6267-0 (pbk.)
1. English language – Study and teaching – Foreign speakers.
2. Second language acquisition. 3. Education, Bilingual. I. Title.

PE1128.A2G673 2010
428.2'4–dc22
                                         2010021262

Typeset by Newgen Imaging Systems Pvt Ltd, Chennai, India
Printed and bound in India by Replika Press Pvt Ltd

Contents

Acknowledgements

Grateful thanks to all colleagues, past and present, in Swansea and in North London, especially members of the former Language and Curriculum Access Service in Enfield who provided many of the examples of classroom activities and stimulated my interest in this area. Thank you to schools in Swansea and Oxford, particularly St Helen's Primary and Cutteslowe Primary, for sharing expertise and providing examples of school and classroom practice and apologies if I have failed to acknowledge examples and activities which I have been using for many years and have lost the original source.

Special thanks to Chris for the drawings and Nicky for the Italian translation and the advice on Chapter 3. Thanks to Tony, as always, for his patience.

Introduction

This book is intended to be helpful to a number of audiences: students in initial teacher education (ITE), newly qualified teachers, teaching assistants (TAs) and teachers who have little experience of working with learners of English as an additional language (EAL). It is also intended to place EAL teaching within the wider spectrum of general everyday teaching and learning in Key Stages 2 and 3 and to demonstrate that while EAL learners have their particular needs these can be catered for, successfully, within the mainstream classroom. Indeed the mainstream classroom is the best place for EAL learners to learn their new language, while they are also learning the concepts, skills and values within the curriculum.

> Language support is best provided within the mainstream classroom wherever possible, as time out of subject lessons for additional language tuition may cause the learner to fall behind in the curriculum. (DfES 2005:5)

The idea for the book arose from involvement in partnership teaching, with language specialists and classroom teachers, while working in a local authority advisory team, followed by twelve years working with students in initial teacher education. It became apparent that despite college based work on inclusive practice, and a focused session on EAL learners led by specialist teachers, many students were quite unsure about how to teach the additional language learners in their school experience classes. It also became apparent that many classroom teachers were unable to give them appropriate support and guidance because they themselves were unsure of what to do for the best.

It is widely accepted that good teaching and learning for EAL pupils is good teaching and learning for all. Walters (2007:153) tells us:

> If you have EAL learners in your classroom then planning to support their language development is a central part of your planning for learning in the classroom. This may sound very daunting but many of the things you plan for and do in your classroom for your EAL learners will benefit all the learners and many of these strategies are ones you may already be aware of.

With this in mind the initial reflections at the beginning of each chapter are intended to raise prior knowledge and experience gained in mainstream classrooms to set the scene for the ideas and issues to follow. Student teachers will be referred to a wider range of standards for qualified teacher status (QTS) than those relating explicitly to EAL learners because these standards refer to all parts of a teacher's practice and to all learners. Standards statements for both England and Wales will be given because although they are similar in intent they are phrased slightly differently.

Terminology

Throughout the book the terms home language and first language will be used interchangeably, and refer to the language customarily spoken in the home and which the child learned first. Pupils will be referred to as additional language learners or EAL learners rather than bilingual learners, although this term is widely used. Additional language learners will be learning bilingually because they will be using two languages, their first language and English in their learning. The term bilingual, in this instance, does not imply equal fluency in both languages.

The book is organized as follows:

Chapter 1: Raising the Issues

A number of important background issues need to be discussed when considering the inclusion of EAL learners in our schools. This chapter sets the scene for the inclusion of EAL learners by looking at the historical development of

EAL teaching and the legislative and population contexts. It also discusses issues of bullying and racism. The United Nations Convention on the Rights of the Child is introduced here, along with the important documents *Every Child Matters* and *Children and Young People: Rights to Action*.

Chapter 2: Language and Identity

The importance of language in our lives cannot be overstated. The relationship between language and identity is complex and an understanding of this complexity is important for teachers of all pupils, including EAL pupils. This chapter will explore some of the aspects of the development and use of language which are relevant to all learners in our primary and secondary schools.

Chapter 3: Language Acquisition

This chapter will give a general outline of first language development and will discuss the different elements of language which are involved in successful communication. It will then look at additional language acquisition and identify some of the similarities and differences.

Chapter 4: A Language Rich Environment

Language is central to learning for all. This chapter explores the idea of a learning environment which is rich in language as a desirable environment for all pupils.

Chapter 5: The Supportive Learning Environment

At the heart of good teaching is an understanding of how to provide a learning environment which genuinely supports the learner. Following on from the language rich environment which supports all learners we explore some of the aspects of the learning environment, in the classroom and school, which have a particular impact on EAL learners.

Chapter 6: Assessment and Planning

All EAL learners need to be assessed on entry to the school in order to determine how best to support them in learning English and in their cognitive development. This chapter briefly discusses initial assessment and then looks at aspects of the summative and formative assessment of EAL learners.

Chapter 7: General Strategies to Support EAL Acquisition

Here we suggest and give classroom examples of general support strategies which can be easily employed by a student or a teacher new to teaching EAL pupils. Most of the strategies are appropriate for pupils in the early stages of English acquisition and can be adapted for primary and secondary school learners.

Chapter 8: Developing Competence In English

Pupils whose English has developed beyond the early stages and whose spoken English is competent for everyday communication will continue to need help to acquire the academic language needed as they move on through secondary school towards GCSE. This chapter will look at some strategies which are simple to organize but will provide the kind of support needed for pupils at this 'developing competency' level.

Chapter 9: End Note

Concluding comments and a checklist of general strategies.

As indicated at the beginning of this introduction each chapter will have a point of reflection to set the scene and it will also have suggestions for further reading and for further enquiries related to the content of the chapter and intended to deepen or extend understanding.

A first reflection exercise

La Rivolta di Boudicca
See Figure 0.1.

- Do you speak or read Italian? If you do not, can you work out what to do with the work sheet which is used in a Year 4 class in their topic on Romans in Britain (in English, of course)?
- How does it make you feel to be faced with a work sheet in a language you do not understand?
- What clues are there on the sheet to help you to understand the content?
- What other help would you need to be able to complete the task?

La Rivolta di Boudicca

Nel 60 dC una tribù Britannica che si chiamava gli Iceni si è rivoltato contro la regola Romana. Sono stati condotti dalla loro regina, Boudicca. Hanno fatto danni terribili ai romani prima che fossero battuti.

Qui sotto sono due descrizioni della regina Boudicca scritte dai storici della storia romana. Usando tutte le informazioni su questa pagina, fai un disegno di Boudicca.

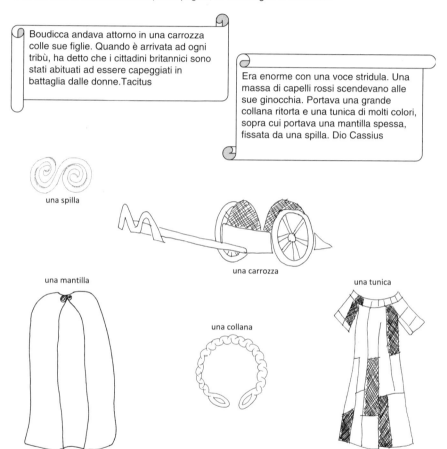

Boudicca andava attorno in una carrozza colle sue figlie. Quando è arrivata ad ogni tribù, ha detto che i cittadini britannici sono stati abituati ad essere capeggiati in battaglia dalle donne.Tacitus

Era enorme con una voce stridula. Una massa di capelli rossi scendevano alle sue ginocchia. Portava una grande collana ritorta e una tunica di molti colori, sopra cui portava una mantilla spessa, fissata da una spilla. Dio Cassius

una spilla

una carrozza

una mantilla

una collana

una tunica

Figure 0.1 Boudicca worksheet

Further reading

Cline, T. and Frederickson, N. (eds) (1996) *Curriculum Related Assessment, Cummins and Bilingual Children.* Cleveden: Multilingual Matters

Cummins, J.(2001) *Negotiating Identities: Education for Empowerment in a Diverse Society.* 2nd Edition. Ontario, CA: California Association for Bilingual Education

Levine, J. (1996) *Developing Pedagogies in the Multilingual Classroom.* Stoke on Trent: Trentham Books

McWilliam, N. (1998) *What's in a Word? Vocabulary Development in Multilingual Classrooms.* Stoke on Trent: Trentham Books

Watkins, C. (2005) *Classrooms as Learning Communities: What's in it for Schools?* London: Routledge

Wray, D. and Lewis, M. (1997) Extending Literacy: Children Reading and Writing Non- Fiction. London: Routledge

Setting the Context and Identifying Issues

This chapter seeks to place the teaching of EAL pupils within a wider context which all classroom practitioners should be aware of. It will consider the legislative framework and aspects of the wider social inclusion agenda which have an impact on schools and provision for additional language learners. Topics will include:

- the historical background to additional language teaching
- the legislative context
- the school context

- issues of race, population distribution and SEN
- Children's Rights
- Every Child Matters and Children and Young People Rights to Action

An understanding of this context will contribute to the following standards:

QTS standards for England

Q3 (b) Be aware of the policies and practices of the workplace and share in collective responsibility for their implementation.

Q21 (a) Be aware of the current legal requirements, national policies and guidance on the safeguarding and promotion of the well-being of children and young people.

QTS standards for Wales

S1.8 They are aware of, and work within, the statutory frameworks relating to teachers' responsibilities.

S2.2 They know and understand the National Curriculum aims and guidelines; in particular, they know and understand the requirements and entitlements set out in the *Including all Learners* statement that appears at the beginning of each National Curriculum subject order and framework.

Reflection

- What do you know about the national policies which underpin school policies and practice relating to the teaching of EAL pupils?

Historical background

It would be useful at the outset to look at how the teaching of EAL pupils has been organized over the last several decades, from pupils being taught in withdrawal units in the 1960s and 70s to all pupils being part of mainstream classrooms as is the practice now. The following summary of the sequence of changes in practice is taken from induction training materials for teaching assistants published by the DfES in 2002:

- Language Centres were established in many LEAs with a view to teaching pupils some English before they went into full-time schooling. They were set up with money made available by the Home Office. English was taught in a de-contextualized way and did not prepare pupils for curriculum content. Pupils were socially and linguistically isolated from their English-speaking peers.

- Language Centres were phased out and the teachers went into schools to offer some English language teaching on site, either in the mainstream classrooms or in withdrawal groups. There were time constraints as the teachers had to travel between schools. English language support was not necessarily linked to the curriculum.
- Language support teachers work in partnership with class and subject teachers, planning curriculum delivery together to enhance the access of pupils learning EAL to subject knowledge, as well as developing their acquisition of the English language. Partnership teaching has helped class and subject teachers plan inclusively for pupils' learning without relying on the presence of a support teacher. This approach works well in schools where time is available for joint planning. It requires language support teachers to develop their subject knowledge, especially at secondary level.
- Language specialist and mainstream teachers plan the inclusive curriculum together. TAs support implementation in the classroom. TAs need to feel confident in supporting pupils' English language acquisition and curriculum learning. They need to be deployed effectively, with full access to lesson plans. (DfES 2002e:7)

We can see from this summary that recommended practice is for partnership teaching between language specialists and classroom teachers, supported by well-trained teaching assistants. These changes in practice are underpinned by a sequence of legislation and influential Government reports:

Summary of key legislation and reports

1966 Section 11 of the Local Government Act 1966 provides additional funding for local government for English language teaching, and is principally geared to teaching children arriving in UK schools from the New Commonwealth.

1975 The Bullock Report, a major report on the teaching of English, promotes the importance of language across the curriculum. It states that 'No child should be expected to cast off the language and culture of the home as (s)he crosses the school threshold'.

1976 The Race Relations Act 1976 makes racial discrimination open to legal challenge.

1981 The Rampton Report attempts to address growing concerns about race relations among parents and communities. It introduces the notion of institutional racism and promotes a programme of 'multi-cultural' education.

1985 The Swann Report focuses attention on linguistic and other barriers that prevent access to education. It implies that the use of separate language centres may be discriminatory in effect as they deny children access to the full range of educational opportunities available.

1988 In the report of a formal investigation in Calderdale LEA, the Commission for Racial Equality (CRE) states that Calderdale's policy of separate English language tuition for ethnic minority pupils cannot be justified on educational grounds and amounts to indirect racial discrimination.

- The National Curriculum states that all pupils are entitled to a broad and balanced curriculum.

1993 A Private Member's bill extends Section 11 funding to include support for all ethnic minority pupils.

1999 The Ethnic Minority Achievement Grant (EMAG) replaces Section 11 funding and places the responsibility for the achievement of ethnic minority pupils on schools.

- The Macpherson Report, following the enquiry into the murder of Stephen Lawrence in 1993 emphasizes the need to address institutional racism. It requires all LEAs, other branches of local government, and the police to make explicit their actions to counter racial discrimination.

2000 The National Curriculum is revised and the duty to ensure teaching is inclusive and is made statutory: 'Teachers have a duty to plan their approaches to teaching and learning so that all pupils can take part in lessons fully and effectively'.

- OFSTED institutes regulatory training for all inspectors in the evaluation of educational inclusion, with a strong emphasis on race issues.
- The Race Relations Amendment Act 2000 requires all public bodies to produce a Race Equality policy by 31 May 2002, and to have explicit means of reporting, monitoring and challenging racial harassment.
- The CRE publication *Learning for All* sets out the standards for Race Equality in schools (DfES 2002e:9).

The legislative context

Education policy in England and Wales reflects the commitment of both the Westminster Government and the Welsh Assembly Government to social justice and inclusion and there is a range of legislation and policy documents which schools need to take into consideration when writing their own policies. The Race Relations Amendment Act (2000) and the Children Act (2004) are two which are particularly relevant here because they directly concern EAL learners. The Special Educational Needs Code of Practice, published in 2001 in England and 2002 in Wales is also relevant, as is the appreciation that the general curriculum requirements, as laid out in the 1988 Education Reform Act, and subsequent Education Acts, apply to all pupils in maintained schools:

General requirements in relation to curriculum

The curriculum for a maintained school or maintained nursery school satisfies the requirements of this section if it is a balanced and broadly-based curriculum which –

   (a) promotes the spiritual, moral, cultural, mental and physical development of pupils at the school and of society, and
   (b) prepares pupils at the school for the opportunities, responsibilities and experiences of later life (Education Reform Act, 1988).

The school context

Most schools and classrooms in the UK today will have pupils for whom English is not their mother tongue. Some will be newly arrived with little or no English and some will have been settled in school for some time and may appear to be fluent in English. All pupils with English as an additional language have particular needs which students and newly qualified teachers and many more experienced colleagues, may find daunting to meet. According to Ferris, Catling and Scott (2002:3), in order to meet the needs of EAL learners all classroom practitioners need to know about:

- The normal development of children's first language and English as an additional language
- The relationship between language and learning
- The languages pupils use, scripts they have experience of and how this experience can be built on in school
- The cultural norms pupils are familiar with and how these might affect teacher judgements
- The role of the first language in children's learning and how bilingual staff can support learning
- The needs of children and parents/carers on admission to a setting
- The links between a child's identity, self esteem, language and culture which are crucial to learning

- The role of literacy in children's development of EAL
- Key teaching strategies to help children acquire another language.

This might seem to be quite a tall order, especially for student teachers when there are so many demands on the initial teacher education (ITE) curriculum. Lack of time in ITE courses, particularly PGCE courses, means that students on school placements and newly qualified teachers in their first posts often have little understanding of additional language learners or awareness of strategies to employ to support their learning. The standards for qualified teacher status (QTS) in England and in Wales show that it is a requirement for student teachers to develop the knowledge and skills to work effectively with EAL learners in order to attain QTS but this is not as daunting as it seems when the knowledge and skills are based firmly in a good understanding of teaching and learning.

School populations

Schools across England and Wales vary greatly in the number of pupils whose first language is not English. Some schools have very few or no EAL learners while in some schools many different languages are spoken and some pupils speak and are literate in several languages when they arrive. Pupils coming into Welsh schools come into a bi-lingual environment and learn both English and Welsh. All of these pupils will be learning the English language at the same time as they are learning the content of the curriculum through the English language.

Some areas of the country have a higher proportion of EAL pupils than others. A glance at Table 1.1 will show the distribution in England in 2008 (based on provisional data).

Within each area of the country there will be differences in the school populations. Some schools, particularly in inner cities, will have a high percentage of EAL pupils speaking a range of different first languages; other schools will have a small number of pupils and the teacher might find that he or she has a single child in the class. The amount of support available from ethnic minority language support teams will also vary from authority to authority but where available this service is invaluable.

The following case studies will give a glimpse of life in two primary schools in different parts of the United Kingdom.

Table 1.1 Percentage of Pupils Whose First Language is Known or Believed to be Other Than English

	Pupils in Maintained Primary Schools	Pupils in Maintained Secondary Schools
England	14.4	10.8
North east	4.7	3.0
North west	10.3	7.1
Yorkshire and The Humber	12.8	9.0
East midlands	9.2	7.0
West Midlands	16.7	12.4
East of England	8.3	5.9
London	42.0	35.4
Inner London	53.6	48.7
Outer London	35.6	29.5
South East	8.1	6.4
South West	3.7	2.7

Source: DCSF (2008), provisional school census data

Data for schools in Wales is not available as it is not collected. It is intended to start collecting school level data in Wales in 2011.

Data for Scotland and N. Ireland is beyond the scope of this book.

Case Study 1: Swansea Primary School

Number of pupils on roll   186.5 (Full Time Equivalent)
Number of EAL pupils   162 (Full Time Equivalent)

First Languages Spoken by Pupils (17)	No. of Pupils
Sylheti/Bengali	137
Hakka	2
Arabic	6
Tamil	2
Cantonese	1
Urdu	4
Hindi	1
Swahili	2
Russian	1

French Creole	2
Latvian	1
Turkish	1
Bisaya/Tagalog	1
Shona	1
Portuguese	1
Chinese	1
Malayan	1

As you can see, the majority of pupils in this school speak Sylheti and Bengali and the school serves the largest Bengali community in Swansea.

Case Study 2: Oxford Primary School

Number of pupils on roll   189 (Full Time Equivalent)
Number of EAL pupils   99 (Full Time Equivalent)

First Languages Spoken by Pupils (23)	No. of Pupils
Bengali	8
Arabic	6
Thai	2
Malayan	4
French	2
Swahili	2
Chinese	3
Chinese/Mandarin	2
Japanese	2
Spanish	1
Turkish	2
Shona	2
Korean	3

Japanese	2
Portuguese	2
Russian	2
Urdu	2
Farsi	1
Marathi	1
Albanian	1
Italian	1
Rny A Kole	1
Polish	2
Georgian	1

This school has quite a different population from the Swansea school, with more languages spoken and no significant majority group. The school population is made up of individual or small groups of families with different language backgrounds. The largest group of pupils in the school speak English as their first language.

The populations of these two schools, of a similar size but different catchments, give an indication of the different situations in schools and therefore the very different environments for learning which will necessarily be developed. The DfES (2002b) outline a number of examples of classrooms which differ in their languages and literacies:

1. A first language shared by a majority which is not English. The Swansea school is an example of this and in such a situation the teacher becomes the principal role model of standard spoken English for the pupils in the class. Although use of the first language will be an essential support for learning it will be important to establish the clear expectation that all pupils will be using English as the target language in the classroom.
2. A first language in common: there are one or two pupils in a class who share a first language. They will be able to support each other's learning by using their first language as a foundation for speaking and writing English.
3. A range of languages and cultures: there are several EAL learners in the class but they are from different language and cultural backgrounds. This situation provides a fruitful opportunity for discussions about how different languages work.

4. 'Isolated learners': the pupil may be the only EAL learner in the class or is the sole speaker of a particular language in the school. In this case it will be easy for the pupil to feel excluded, unless given particular support, and it may take some time for the pupil to become sufficiently confident to say anything in English. However, we do know that a silent period is not unusual and is not usually a cause for concern unless there are other indications that the pupil is not settling in (adapted from DfES 2002b:6).

SEN/EAL confusion

It is possible for any teacher, especially an inexperienced one or a student, to confuse poor language skills with cognitive difficulties but it is important to make a clear distinction between EAL pupils and those with special educational needs. As stated in the 1996 Education Act, which reiterates the 1981 and subsequent Acts:

A child must not be regarded as having a learning difficulty solely because the language or form of the language of the home is different from the language in which he or she will be taught. (1996 Education Act, in DfES 2005:9)

If a pupil learning English as an additional language is thought to have special educational needs, having been carefully assessed (see Chapter 6), then teachers, specialist language staff and the SEN coordinator can work together to arrange appropriate support for learning. Gifted and talented pupils with EAL needs also need to be recognized and must not be held back from learning by being grouped with the less able pupils in the classroom, a distressing but all too common practice.

Is EAL a racial issue?

It can sometimes be the case, particularly in predominantly white contexts, that student teachers regard addressing the needs of minority ethnic pupils and those with English as an additional language as less of a priority than other aspects of their training. The Race Relations Amendment Act (2000) requires schools and teachers to deliver curricula which actively promote 'race' equality and challenge racism and as we saw above English language teaching which is not appropriately organized can be seen as racial discrimination.

Since 2002 there has been a statutory requirement for every school to have a race- equality policy and every member of staff, including students and TAs should be familiar with it. There is no space here to discuss this further but there are several useful documents to help schools to write policy; see in the further reading section below, and the Government Standards Website which is a useful source of information: http://www.standards.dcsf.gov.uk/ethnicminorities/faqs/raceequality/

Inclusion and children's rights

Removing barriers to learning and giving all children the opportunity to learn as well as they can are fundamental aims of an inclusive education system. Underpinning the concept of inclusion in UK schools is the most important statement on children's rights to be developed by the international community: the United Nations Convention on the Rights of the Child (UNCRC). This convention, presented to the United Nations General Assembly in 1989 and ratified by every nation in the world, except the USA and Somalia (at the time of writing), sets out the 42 rights for all children and young people up to the age of eighteen and how these rights should be implemented. The rights fall broadly into four categories: survival rights, protection rights, development rights and participation rights. Harrison (2008:8) groups the rights in a way which gives us a good idea of the range involved in the convention:

- Rights to equality
- Rights to family care
- Rights to survival and development
- Rights to identity and expression
- Rights for refugee children
- Rights for children with disabilities
- Rights to health care and economic security
- Rights to education and leisure
- Rights to protection and from harmful work
- Rights to protection from abuse and torture
- Rights to rehabilitation
- Rights to justice

Our schools and educational settings, along with other services such as the National Health Service and Local Authority Social Services, have the responsibility of meeting children's needs in each of these categories. The Children Act (2004) and the associated *Every Child Matters* documents address the range of services and provision for children and young people. The values inherent in the UNCRC form the basis for these documents although the rights themselves are not explicitly stated.

The Children Act and *Every Child Matters*

The Government Green paper, *Every Child Matters*, was published in 2003 followed by the Children Act in 2004. The purpose of these policy documents was to improve and strengthen children's services and they were followed by a series of further documents, each focusing on a particular section of services to children and young people. The following extract is from *Every Child Matters: Change for Children in Schools*, DfES (2004b).

> *Every Child Matters*, the Government's vision for children's services, was published in September 2003. It proposed reshaping children's services to help achieve the outcomes children and young people told us are key to well-being in childhood and later life:
>
> • Be healthy
> • Stay safe
> • Enjoy and achieve
> • Make a positive contribution
> • Achieve economic well-being

The Government has legislated for changes in the way children's services work together. *Every Child Matters: Change for Children* explains how the new Children Act 2004 forms the basis of a long-term programme of change. This document is one of a series that describe the implications for different services. All of these documents and others referred to in the text are available at www.everychildmatters.gov.uk. Whether you are a head teacher, a teacher, a teaching assistant, a member of the support staff or a governor, everyone in a school has a role to play. DfES (2004b:1)

UNCRC in Wales: *Children and Young People: Rights to Action*

Since devolution in 1999 policy regarding children and young people in Wales has steadily diverged from policy in England. In 2004, the Welsh Assembly

Government formally adopted the UNCRC and produced a document for Wales, equivalent to *Every Child Matters* in England. This document is explicitly based on the UNCRC and is called *Children and Young People: Rights to Action* (WAG:2004). Two extracts are below:

UN convention on the rights of the child

1. The Assembly Government has adopted the UN Convention on the Rights of the Child (Annex 1) as the basis of all our work for children and young people in Wales. We have translated this into seven Core Aims through which we will work to ensure that all children and young people:

   - have a flying start in life;
   - have a comprehensive range of education and learning opportunities;
   - enjoy the best possible health and are free from abuse, victimization and exploitation;
   - have access to play, leisure, sporting and cultural activities;
   - are listened to, treated with respect and have their race and cultural identity recognized;
   - have a safe home and a community which supports physical and emotional well-being;
   - are not disadvantaged by poverty.

   (WAG 2004:1)

2. In preparing their Frameworks, Partnerships are asked to *"recognize the importance of culture and first language in Wales"*, and this requirement will be taken account of in the assessment of plans. This includes issues relating to the Welsh language and culture and also extends to other languages and cultures. Wales has a wide variety of cultures, and services need to be planned to recognize cultural differences and to deliver in different languages where appropriate.

   (Ibid:10)

The principles and values set out in *Children and Young People: Rights to Action* apply to all children's and young people's services in Wales, just as *Every Child Matters* applies to all services in England. However, the language of children's rights is explicit in the Welsh documentation while implicit in the English. In the recent revision of the National Curriculum in Wales all curriculum documents explicitly refer to the UNCRC in their value statements. Implicit references to *Children and Young People: Rights to Action* are also easy to identify, as the following extract from the *Personal and Social Education Framework for 7–19 Year Olds in Wales*, shows:

Including all learners
Responsibilities of schools, colleges and other learning providers

Under the United Nations Convention on the Rights of the Child and the Welsh Assembly Government's overarching strategy document *Rights to Action,* all children and young people must be provided with an education which develops their personality and talents to the full. The Education Act 2002 further strengthens schools' duty to safeguard and promote the welfare of all children and young people.

The equal opportunities legislation which covers age, disability, gender, race, religion and belief and sexual orientation further places a duty on learning providers in Wales towards present and prospective learners to eliminate discrimination and harassment, to promote positive attitudes and equal opportunities and to encourage participation.

Learning providers should develop in every learner a sense of personal and cultural identity that is receptive and respectful towards others. They should plan across the curriculum to develop the knowledge and understanding, skills, values and attitudes that will enable learners to participate in our multi-ethnic society in Wales. Learning providers should develop approaches that support the ethnic and cultural identities of all learners and reflect a range of perspectives, to engage learners and prepare them for life as global citizens.

Learning providers must work to reduce environmental and social barriers to inclusion and offer opportunities for all learners to achieve their full potential in preparation for further learning and life. Where appropriate, learning providers will need to plan and work with specialist services to ensure relevant and accessible learning experiences. For learners with disabilities in particular, they should:

- improve access to the curriculum
- make physical improvements to increase participation in education
- provide information in appropriate formats.

Learning providers should seek advice regarding reasonable adjustments, alternative/adapted activities and appropriate equipment and resources which may be used to support the full participation of all learners, including those who use a means of communication other than speech.

For learners whose first language is neither English nor Welsh, learning providers should take specific action to help them learn both English and Welsh through the curriculum. They should provide learners with material that is appropriate to their ability, previous education and experience and which extends their language development. They should also encourage the use of learners' home languages for learning.

(DCELLS: 2008:6)

Key Points

This chapter has set out some of the wider context in which our schools operate and has introduced, briefly, some of the legislation and policy documents which teachers need to be aware of, in general and when making provision for EAL learners. The chapter suggests that it would be useful for students and teachers to be familiar with some of the following documents:

- The Race Relations Amendment Act (2000)
- The Children Act (2004)
- Every Child Matters: Change for Children in Schools
- Children and Young People: Rights to Action
- The United Nations Convention on the Rights of the Child

Moving on: suggestions for further enquiry

- How many EAL learners are there in your school? How many first languages are spoken and what are they?
- To what extent are you and your colleagues aware of the United Nations Convention on the Rights of the Child?
- Do you know about the five outcomes of *Every Child Matters* or the seven core aims of *Children and Young People: Rights to Action*? Are they reflected in any of your policy documents?

Further reading

- A simple background to development of the UNCRC can be found in Harrison, D. (2008) *Regardless of Frontiers: Children's Rights and Global Learning.* Stoke on Trent: Trentham Books
- For further information about the UNCRC and other relevant matters go to www. Unicef.org
- Further information on *Every Child Matters* can be found at www.everychildmatters.gov.uk. The document *Children and Young People: Rights to Action* is available at http://wales.gov.uk/docrepos/40382/40382313/childrenyoungpeople/consultation/rightstoaction

- Support for writing a school racial equality policy can be found in: CRE (2002) *Framework for a Race Equality Policy for Schools.* Available at: http://www.equalityhumanrights.com/uploaded_files/PSD/52_framework_schools.pdf
- An interesting and useful discussion of equality issues in education can be found in: Richardson, R. (2005) *Race Equality & Education.* London: ATL. Available at: http://www.atl.org.uk/publications-and-resources/education-publications/race-equality-education.asp

Language and Identity 2

This chapter will consider some of the factors linking language and identity. Topics addressed will include the following:

- The relationship between language and identity
- Issues of racism and bullying involving language
- Monolingualism and multilingualism
- Home language and home/school links

A number of standards for QTS will be addressed throughout the chapter.

QTS standard for England

Q18. Understand how children and young people develop and that the progress and well-being of learners are affected by a range of developmental, social, religious, ethnic, cultural and linguistic influences.

QTS standard for Wales

S2.4 They understand how learners' physical, intellectual, linguistic, social, cultural and emotional development can affect their learning.

The discussion of racism and bullying and the importance of home language and culture will contribute to other standards and these will be given in the relevant sections.

Reflection

- How many languages do you speak? Are you literate in more than one language? Would you say you were bi-lingual? Multilingual? What do these languages mean to you as a person? How do they contribute to your sense of who you are, your identity?
- Perhaps you are literate in one language, English. Do you speak in the same way to your tutor or head teacher as you do to your friends? Do you use a different 'language', albeit a variety of English, in different situations? Do your different 'varieties of English' correspond to different aspects of your identity?
- Think about people you have met from other countries and cultures. What do they do differently from you? Might any of these differences affect their children in school?

Relationship between language and identity

The formation of an individual's identity is a complex process involving many factors and continuing throughout life. Major influences are race, gender and social class and these overlap and interact in complex ways. Siraj-Blatchford and Clarke (2000) discuss the concept of identity formation and provide a number of useful references for further reading relating to race, gender and class. Their book, *Supporting Identity, Diversity and Language in the Early Years,* focuses, as the title suggests, on early years education but there is a great deal which is relevant to older pupils both in primary and secondary schools. Language and literacy cannot be separated from race, gender and social class and the importance of language in the development of a cultural identity cannot be underestimated.

The way we speak and write influences how others perceive us, and the way other people speak to us affects how we see ourselves, our identity. The language we use, and hear and see around us, relates closely to our personal identity, to cultural identification and to attitudes and beliefs that may influence the way we learn. Snow (1992) tells us that some pupils can feel that their personal identity is threatened if they become too good a speaker of the new language and she makes two interesting points that further underline the complexity of the relationship between language and identity:

(a) an additional language which has negative associations for the learner is unlikely to be easy to learn and
(b) good grammar and a perfect accent may not result in good communication

Siraj-Blatchford (1994, in Siraj-Blatchford and Clarke, 2000:10) gives an interesting and rather distressing example of how negative attitudes to a particular language, spoken or written, can influence even small children. She tells the story of Amar who is three and a half years old and who declares 'I'm not putting my wellies into that bag, it's got Paki writing on it'. This small child has already learned that there are different forms of written language and that his home language is not valued by some of the people around him who are important to him. Already he is rejecting a part of his home culture. How will this affect his identity as a child of Pakistani origin?

The story of Amar is an example of how social and cultural pressures affect learners in situations where different social value is attached to their two languages (Snow 1992). Snow's study discusses immigrant families in the USA and Canada and explores reasons why their children learn English so quickly and so well and risk losing their native language. In some states in the USA there are 'two-way' bilingual programmes for speakers of Spanish and English. She notes that in these programmes Spanish speakers learn English faster than English speakers learn Spanish and suggests that perhaps even kindergarten-aged children are well aware of society's negative evaluation of Spanish speakers. This would bear out Amar's response above.

The language we use is such an important part of who we are that it is not surprising that learning a language is an extremely complex process, involving many factors. When we think about pupils learning a new language in school we need to take account of the factors which influence learning. Affective factors such as self-esteem, peer-perception and respect and cultural identity (SCAA 1996) can help or hinder the learning process as they are intimately bound up with self-perception and identity.

Racism and bullying

At this point it is useful to consider the question of racist attitudes and bullying as they may relate to some EAL pupils. The following standards for QTS are relevant here:

QTS standards for England

Q3 (b) Be aware of the policies and practices of the workplace and share in collective responsibility for their implementation.

Q 21 (a) Be aware of the current legal requirements, national policies and guidance on the safeguarding and promotion of the well-being of children and young people.

QTS standard for Wales

S3.3.14 They recognize and respond effectively to social inclusion and equal opportunities issues as they arise in the classroom, including by challenging stereotyped views, and by challenging bullying or harassment, following relevant policies and procedures.

We are all aware of racist and sexist language and the damaging effect it has upon pupils on the receiving end of such language. We could also reflect upon the effect that attitudes demonstrated by such language might have upon the pupils who use it and where and how they acquire the language and attitudes. There are several studies e.g. Troyna and Hatcher (1991) which investigate sexist and racist behaviour and attitudes in primary schools. These studies show that the links between racist behaviour and bullying seem obvious but they are not always straightforward. The DCSF in England (DCSF, 2007) and the National Assembly for Wales (NAW, 2003) have both produced useful documents to support schools in developing anti-bullying policies and putting their policies into practice. The Welsh document is particularly aware of the importance of language in relation to bullying:

At the outset, it is important to recognize, when establishing a whole-school policy that a number of children and/or their parents will require additional language support whether this is Welsh or other languages. It is necessary to show sensitivity regarding linguistic and bilingual matters when dealing with bullying in schools. Any anti-bullying policy drawn up by schools will need to conform to the Welsh Language Act and should ensure that consideration is given to the linguistic needs of pupils where English is not their first language or not the first language of their parents. (NAW, 2003:2)

Both documents draw the distinction between racism and bullying and point out that there is a difference. The DCSF (2007) document offers the following definition of racist bullying in the section *Safe to Learn: Bullying Around Race Religion and Culture:*

The term racist bullying refers to a range of hurtful behaviour, both physical and psychological, that makes a person feel unwelcome, marginalised, excluded, powerless or worthless because of their colour, ethnicity, culture, faith community, national origin or national status.

and goes on to say that:

While all occurrences of racist bullying are racist incidents, not all of the latter necessarily amount to bullying.

The Welsh document takes a more descriptive, and perhaps wider approach and tells us:

Racist bullying is bullying of children on the grounds of their race, colour, nationality, ethnic or national origin and includes bullying of Roma Gypsy children, children who are Travellers of Irish Heritage, children from Scotland, England and Ireland. In racist bullying, a child is targeted on the basis of their colour or ethnic origin. Bullying of an individual child can have a negative impact on other children of a similar colour or ethnicity, who may perceive themselves as potential targets of similar bullying within the school. Racist bullying is therefore likely to hurt not only the victim, but also other pupils from the same group, and their families. (NAW, 2003:11)

Like the DCSF document it goes to say:

It is important however that all school staff are aware that racism is not the same as bullying. Racism is much broader and takes many forms of which bullying is just one. (Ibid)

Chapter 1 gives some further reading on Racial Policies, and guidance documents for developing Anti-Bullying Policies will be found at the end of this chapter. It is important for all members of staff, including student teachers, to be aware of and to work to put their school policies in practice. Policies set out the vision for a school's ethos and the policies guiding racial and bullying issues are important in setting a school's ethos which is inclusive and promotes equality of opportunity. The following list of issues relating to the attainment of minority ethnic pupils, set out in a Teacher Training Agency Handbook for trainers, indicates the implications of inequalities, including racial, and the importance of successfully implemented policies to the ethos of a school and therefore to the achievement of its pupils.

Raising the attainment of minority ethnic pupils

Ethos and practices of the school

Some issues to consider:

- inequality can operate at institutional, cultural, individual levels – how do successful schools and teachers counter this?
- racial equality is an issue for all schools including those with mainly White population
- the importance of ethnic minority staff to ethos of school
- prejudice and discrimination can affect emotional, social and intellectual development of all pupils
- what constitutes racial bullying and harassment? What impact does this have on pupil attainment and life of school?
- racial taunting is a daily experience for many and can start in nursery and continue through school life
- successful implementation of school policies on equality and social justice are central to education which promotes attainment for all pupils
- inclusive schools counter stereotyping, racist bullying and harassment by:

  - stating in policy documents that these are unacceptable attitudes and will not be tolerated
  - creating an ethos in which these issues can be openly discussed by the whole school community
  - implementing, monitoring, reviewing procedures for dealing with racist behaviour

   – having an inclusive curriculum and resources, and expectation of equitable treatment for all members of school community

- pupils need support to deal with racist incidents – they need to be taught strategies to deal where there is little support
- stereotyping pupils can result in depressed expectations, low self-esteem and under-achievement
- inclusive schools respect pupils' identities
- inclusive schools monitor and use data on attendance, lateness, behaviour, exclusion in order to inform strategies
- because of mobility some pupils e.g. asylum seekers, Travellers and some pupils with English as an additional language may need to become familiar with school language, customs, rules. (TTA, Raising the Attainment of Minority Ethnic Pupils: Guidance and resource materials for initial teacher trainers)

Monolingual or multilingual?

English people are notorious for their disinclination to learn other languages. This trait is not shared by the majority of other peoples in the world, or indeed in the UK. An increasing number of people in Wales are bi-lingual and conduct their daily lives in English and Welsh according to need and all children in Wales learn Welsh as part of the National Curriculum, as a first language or as an additional language depending upon the school. Informal surveys carried out among Welsh ITE students suggest that the Welsh language is probably the most important contributor to the Welsh identity, even for those who do not speak it well.

Speaking two languages or more can be seen as an extension of what all monolingual people do when they make use of the variability within a language. English is a particularly rich language in this respect as even everyday vocabulary has a range of available synonyms from different linguistic roots and we all know ways using different words to make ourselves sound more or less 'clever'. We all adjust our vocabulary, grammar and phraseology to suit the situation we are in. If we are socially aware, and most of us are, we might express anger or pain to a friend by the use of a colourful expletive but in the presence of a child, or perhaps one's mother, we might choose a more moderate expression. In the same way, a bilingual or multilingual person would say 'thank you' to an English speaker, 'diolch' to a Welsh speaker and 'merci' to a French speaker. Adjusting our language in this way reflects our relationship with the person we are speaking to. It is also a reflection of our identity, who we are and how we wish to be seen.

The advantages of bilingualism and multilingualism are widely acknowledged. Many people used to think, and some still do, that young children will be confused by learning and using more than one language. This is manifestly not the case as Kenner (2004) demonstrates in her book *Becoming Biliterate: Young Children Learning Different Writing Systems*. Here we find examples of children operating in two or more spoken languages, for example Gujarati, Urdu and English; Spanish and English; Mandarin, Cantonese and English. The young children she describes are also beginning to write their languages, which may involve a different script system as in Chinese languages and Arabic. Far from being confused the children in her study are very positive and enjoy their languages, and share their enjoyment with classmates. She tells us:

> Teachers and parents sometimes think that young children will be confused if they are dealing with more than one writing system. However, children have many more capabilities than we realize. They are constantly investigating the written world around them, finding out what graphic symbols stand for and how they can be used to communicate with others. (Kenner 2004:x)

The parents of many of our immigrant pupils understand the advantages and importance of bilingualism in maintaining the cultural connection with their families and communities. They also appreciate that being able to operate in more than one language system helps to develop the flexible identity and wider communication skills which are so useful in the world today.

Conteh and Begum (2006) describe a 'bilingual approach' to learning, involving general language awareness and the effective use of bilingual support. They explain that it can be used by all teachers, including monolingual English, and is valuable for all learners for a number of reasons:

- All pupils need to have the ability to analyse and compare languages. This will increase their language awareness and their cognitive capacity.
- Talking and thinking about different languages will improve communication between pupils of different language and cultural backgrounds.
- Promoting a positive ethos, which nurtures language diversity, contributes to overcoming conflict in school and even in the wider community. (Conteh and Begum, 2006:63,64)

Importance of home language and culture – 'more than just words'

When families emigrate and go to live in a new country they take with them their language, of course, and also the cultural roles and child-rearing practices they have experienced themselves. These may be minimally different, as with an American family who may notice that there are some differences in word use such as 'yard' rather than 'garden' or 'trunk' instead of 'car boot' but whose language and most child-rearing practices are shared. Alternatively a family from Pakistan or Cyprus will not only have a new language to learn but may also have different expectations of how to raise their children, according to the cultural experiences of the parents.

Examples of difficulties caused by different parental expectations are cited by Siraj-Blatchford and Clarke (2004:92) who discuss the work of Gonzales-Mena (1998). This important study focuses on approaches to child-rearing which relate to independence and interdependence. Gonzales-Mena suggests that one of the main tasks of parents is to not only help their children to become independent individuals but also to establish connections with other people. Different cultures place different emphases on these two important aspects of development, and difficulties may arise when parents' expectations do not match school expectations, particularly in the early years. Parents whose culture places high value on interdependence and family connections may be concerned that their children are being encouraged to be too independent, such as some of the parents from the Bangladeshi community in Swansea who are reluctant to send their small children to nursery because they feel that small children should be cared for in the home.

Different cultures operate different rules about how language is used, for instance who speaks to whom and in what tone; how adults address children and vice versa; whether one makes eye contact when speaking. Parental expectations, determined by culture, will be transmitted to their children and the children will apply the rules to their new language as well as to their first language. This observance of cultural norms will have an influence on who they talk and listen to and on the topics of their conversation and will necessarily have an impact upon their school lives.

Pupils arrive in our classrooms with varying degrees of competence in English and in their mother tongue. They may be from refugee families, bringing with them the effects of a troubled and even traumatic arrival in the country and the disruption of their schooling. They may be the first generation of their family to attend school in the UK and learn English or they may be from long-established minority ethnic groups and be familiar with the school system and with the English language. Pupils will come from a wide range of cultural backgrounds: Bangladeshi, Chinese, Polish, Slovakian, Russian, Iranian, for example. They might be fluent in their use of spoken English or they could be at a very early stage of English acquisition. Some pupils will be literate in their first language while others will not and this will have a marked effect upon their learning of English.

Pupils who are literate in their mother tongue will already have an understanding of how written language works i.e. that it does not always use the same structures as spoken language, that there are rules such as spelling patterns and that there is a correspondence between symbols and sounds when de-coding written text. Leung (2001) points out that transfer of literacy skills from a pupil's mother tongue into English will depend upon the similarities and differences between the two languages and also between the two cultures. He argues strongly for the promotion of pupils' first language in order to develop a good knowledge of the language and also to develop an understanding of where English operates differently. Some EAL pupils will be able to attend a community school in their first language. These schools help to provide the language development and cultural enrichment that makes such a positive contribution to the personal development of their pupils.

Importance of home/school links

QTS standard for England

> Q 5 Recognize and respect the contribution that colleagues, parents and carers can make to the development and well-being of children and young people, and to raising their levels of attainment.

QTS standard for Wales

> S1.4 They recognize the importance of communicating information and expectations clearly and sensitively to parents and guardians and of fostering positive relationships between home and school.

Home-school links are important for all learners. Good home-school links are an indicator of inclusive practise in schools and as such are reported on in inspections by Ofsted and Estyn. In order to provide a positive learning environment for the pupils in our schools we need to be aware of the diversity of cultural backgrounds of the families who make up our school community. These families may be predominantly white English or Welsh but with diverse social backgrounds and therefore expectations, or they may be a mixture of different ethnic backgrounds with the concomitant language and cultural differences. An awareness of this diversity and a willingness to work with parents and families is important to the personal and social development of pupils. The DfES has issued guidance for schools on supporting ethnic minority pupils and gives the following advice about working with parents:

Contacts and links with parents

17. Educating pupils with English as an additional language is not a one-way process. Schools have much to gain from the experiences and understandings of pupils, their families and communities. Drawing on their funds of knowledge enriches a school in a range of valuable ways.
18. When admitting a pupil who has recently arrived from another country, schools should gather information about the pupil's linguistic and educational background, for example whether he or she is literate in language(s) other than English and the extent and scope of their previous education. It is valuable to have information about the features of pupils' first languages as well as background information on different education systems and ways in which their culture and educational background may influence learning.
19. If appropriate, schools should send communications to parents in their home language. More generally, it is vital to maintain home-school links with the parents and carers of pupils new to English, using bilingual staff if possible. (DfES 2004a:10)

The following case study illustrates some of the ways a school can work with parents and families to build up positive relationships. The school uses a number of strategies and activities to encourage parents to work in partnership with the school staff.

Case Study: Swansea Primary School

Parent partnerships

- A number of adult learning classes are provided in school:

  > adult literacy,
  > adult IT classes and cyber café,
  > sewing classes
  > family learning group
  > language and play group.

- There is a monthly parents' coffee morning with the specialist language support teacher.
- A PTA meeting is held in school in each half term.
- There are no parents' evenings but parent consultation is conducted over 3 weeks and every parent is contacted. Staff cover for each other using PPA time and after school where necessary.
- There is a parents' section on the school website.
- There are parent notice boards in both infant and junior yards.
- There is a parent suggestions box and a range of useful leaflets for parents such as holiday forms and 'help your child with potty training', in the school foyer.
- A video for parents explains the implications of extended holidays, which happen fairly frequently, and children are given a holiday pack of work to take. Catch up lessons are organized by the language support teacher when pupils return.
- The school uses Parentmail (e-communication) and text messages to communicate more frequently with parents but texts and email do not replace letters and newsletters.
- For important information needing a meeting the school holds 3 meetings in a day, one with translator. Any parent who does not attend is contacted.
- A Traffic Light system to tape record parent messages that require translation is used when necessary – red light requires urgent translation, amber needs a reply within a day or two and green is not urgent – and depending upon the urgency of the message the school is able to play the message down the phone to an off-site translator.
- The school has an allotment for parents as part of its 'Secret Garden' of class allotments.
- The nursery teacher makes home visits before children are due to start school. She takes books and toys and leaves a picture of herself for the child and parents.

This particular school has strong links with the local faith communities and prides itself on its inclusive ethos. Some of its practices will be referred to in later chapters.

Key Points

- The relationship between language and identity is very strong
- It is important to make a distinction between racist language and racist bullying. Ethnic minority pupils may be the focus of either and schools must have policies to deal both bullying and racist incidents.
- A good relationship between school and home and an appreciation of cultural differences is essential.

Moving on: suggestions for further enquiry

- Check/evaluate your school's anti-bullying policy with particular reference to minority groups.

These publications will help:

NAW (2003) *Respecting Others: Anti-Bullying Guidance Circular 23/2003*. Cardiff: NAW. Available at: http://new.wales.gov.uk/topics/educationandskills/policy_strategy_and_planning/schools/

DCSF (2007) *Safe to Learn: Embedding Anti-bullying Work in Schools*. London: DCSF. Available at: http://www.teachernet.gov.uk/wholeschool/behaviour/tacklingbullying/safetolearn/

- How does the school encourage and foster parental involvement in general and with families of EAL pupils in particular? (Talk to mentor/member of staff responsible/governor). What do other schools in the area do?

Further reading

Conteh, J. (2003) *Succeeding in Diversity – Culture Language and Learning in the Primary Classroom*. Stoke on Trent: Trentham Books

Elton-Chalcraft, S. (2009) *It's Not Just About Black and White, Miss: Children's Awareness of Race*. Stoke on Trent: Trentham Books

Ladson-Billings, G. and Gillborn, D. (2004) *The RoutledgeFalmer Reader in Multi-cultural Education*. London: RoutledgeFalmer

Richardson. R. and Wood, A. (1999) *Inclusive Schools, Inclusive Society*. Stoke: Trentham Books

3 Language Acquisition

This chapter will provide a brief introduction to the acquisition of first and additional languages and it will explore some of the factors involved in becoming fluent in both a first and an additional language. There will be four main sections:

- First language development
- Processes involved in communication
- Learning an additional language
- Writing systems

The subject matter and issues raised will contribute to the following standards for QTS which, as you will see, are a combination of subject specific and professional development statements.

QTS standards for England

Q7 Reflect on and improve their practice, and take responsibility for identifying and meeting their developing professional needs.
  (b) Identify priorities for their early professional development in the context of induction.

Q18 Understand how children and young people develop and that the progress and well-being of learners are affected by a range of developmental, social, religious, ethnic, cultural and linguistic influences.

QTS standards for Wales

S1.1 They understand the diverse learning needs of pupils and endeavour to provide the best possible education for them to maximize their potential, whatever their individual aspirations, personal circumstances or cultural, linguistic, religious and ethnic backgrounds.

S1.7 They are able to contribute to the wider development of the school and profession and are aware of the importance of maintaining up-to-date professional knowledge, understanding and skills and are able to reflect on their own practice. They recognize their own needs and take responsibility for their continuing professional development.

Reflection

What do we mean by language and what is the relationship between language and the more complex concept of communication? Thompson (2003:47) gives us a simple working definition of language: 'Language is the ability to understand and use a structured system of sounds and words for communication.'

- What do you understand by the term 'language'?
- What do you think we mean when we talk about communication?
- Do you think we need language in order to communicate?

Developing language

Unless there is a specific learning difficulty all children acquire a first language through social interaction with parents and carers and later with the wider community and their peers. Babies are 'programmed' to respond to their parents and carers from soon after birth and they recognize and pay attention to familiar voices. This attention to voice is one of the first steps in the complex process of acquiring language. All children follow the same developmental sequence but, as we would expect, there are individual differences in how quickly they progress from one stage to the next and in how competent they are at each stage.

Sequence of language development

Table 2.1 shows the sequence of first language development which most children can be expected to follow. Of course, every child is different and is impossible to put an exact age to each stage.

Table 2.1 Sequence of First Language Development

1 month	Shows preference for faces over objects Two-way interactions (proto-conversations) Startled by sudden noises
8 weeks	Responds differently to sounds of own language Coos responsively to parents' talk
3–4 months	Delighted vocalization when spoken to or pleased Can distinguish own language from other similar languages e.g. Spanish and Catalan
6 months	Babbling Different reactions to tone and facial expression Evidence of 'theory of mind' (see below): looks to adults for clues about how to react
9 months	Shouts to attract attention Understands 'no' and 'bye bye'
1 year	Produces variety of sounds associated with the home environment Takes turns in conversations with adults Uses gestures to communicate Responds to own name
12–18 months	First words Joins words together
18 months	Expressive use of 6–20 words Attempts to sing Imitates words Understands simple instructions
2–4 years	'explosion' of naming words; Development of sentences and the generalizing of grammatical rules (e.g. 'foots' instead of 'feet') Vocabulary increasingly intelligible Able to describe past and present experiences Listens to and tells long stories
5 years	Most children have mastered the basics and understand the use of everyday language. Understanding of more complex or abstract words takes time to develop. Speech phonetically correct (except s-f-th)
3–6 years	Continues to develop conversation skills Conversations with older children and adults help to develop questioning Develops social skills and cultural norms of their language Learns different ways of talking for different occasions and formal and informal language.

Source: Adapted from Ripley et al 2001, Sheridan 1997 and Siraj-Blatchford and Clarke 2000

In their training materials for TAs the DfES (2002e) tell us that first language learning normally takes place in a stress-free, family environment where the rules of language are modelled naturally by fluent speakers. In the family context caring adults talk to their children, praise and expand their attempts at speech and reinforce spoken words by gesture, body language and facial expression. Parents and carers use songs, rhymes and games and provide experiences which stimulate language. Siraj-Blatchford and Clarke (2000) also remind us that through this interaction with adults in their family, children not only learn the words and grammar of their first language but also the values and beliefs of their community.

Processes involved in communication

The effective use of language to communicate is a complex process. In order to communicate effectively a person must be able to understand what others are saying (receptive language) and be able to express themselves in a way that others can understand (expressive language). This involves learning about and being able to use a number of different elements of a language system:

- The sounds of the language (phonology)
- The words (vocabulary) and their meanings (semantics)
- The way the words are put together into phrases and sentences (grammar)
- The way sentences are ordered (discourse)
- The appropriate use of the language (pragmatics)

The ability to operate these integral parts of the language system is essential for successful communication and in modern society is essential for successful educational achievement. To communicate well it is also necessary to have an awareness of other people, their interests and perspectives, an ability which Frith (1989 in Ripley et al 2001:2) called 'Theory of Mind'. Awareness of others and their perspectives usually begins to appear at about six months of age (see Table 2.1) but it takes time to develop fully. Many people, especially those on the autistic spectrum, have problems because of poor development in this aspect of communication.

Everyone who learns another language, for any reason, needs to master the elements listed above if they want to be able to use that language effectively. It is also important for teachers of additional language learners to be aware of these different elements and the implications for pupils learning English, so that they can have a better understanding of their pupils and their needs.

Phonology

It is obvious that pupils will need to learn the sounds of English which may be similar, or not, to the sounds in their first language. There may be some sounds which they cannot detect, for example a young man whose first language is Swiss German and whose understanding of English is excellent cannot differentiate between the sound of 'th' in' this' (phonetic symbol θ) and the 'th' in' thief' (phonetic symbol ð). For pupils who are literate in their first language, teachers and other staff also need to be aware that the way sounds are represented in writing may be different in their first language. Not only might the alphabet be different, as in the Cyrillic alphabet in Russian, but the writing system might be completely different as in Chinese or Japanese. We will return to these points later in the chapter.

Vocabulary/Semantics

Learning words and their meanings might seem quite straightforward but English is a particularly complex language with many synonyms and homonyms, and education is a complex context with many sets of specialized vocabulary. It is important always to remember that EAL pupils are learning the English language but they are also learning the curriculum through English and they need to be able to use the appropriate vocabulary for the different curriculum areas. Simple examples are 'table' which has an everyday use as a piece of furniture and a mathematical/scientific use as a method of data presentation, and 'sink' which is an item of household equipment and a verb meaning 'to drop down' which they will meet in science in the context of 'floating and sinking'.

Grammar/Discourse

Putting words together in phrases and sentences, and the appropriate use of word order, verb placement, tense, verb and noun agreement and so on also differs from language to language. Learning to construct correct, grammatical sentences and going on to put these sentences together into an appropriately constructed discussion is an important academic skill and one which many first language English speakers find difficult to master. In order to achieve academically all pupils need to develop their skills in grammar and discourse and they are areas where additional language learners, even when they appear to be fluent in everyday English, will need continuing support.

Pragmatics

The correct use of language, including how familiar or formal to be when speaking, mode of address according to the person being spoken to and appropriate style of writing to suit the occasion, is an important social skill. Customs and norms regarding spoken language vary in different cultures and in different social groups. A simple example is that of making eye contact: some pupils may not be aware that it is customary in our society to look at the person who is speaking, or they may feel uncomfortable because it is regarded as impolite in their culture for a young person to look at an adult who is speaking to them. Teachers and other staff need to be aware of such cultural differences so that they do not misinterpret the behaviour of a recently arrived pupil. It is also important to appreciate that it will take time for a pupil to become accustomed to the norms of communication in English.

Theory of mind

We can assume that most new pupils will have reached the developmental stage where they have an awareness of other people and their perspectives. It might be that if an EAL pupil consistently fails to demonstrate this awareness then it could be a sign of additional learning needs rather than language support needs. In this case the pupil will need to be assessed, initially by the SEN coordinator and then by other experts such as a specialist in English as an additional language or a speech and language therapist.

Learning an additional language

Young children starting school in the Foundation Stage (England) or Foundation Phase (Wales) will have acquired the basics of language in the home and they will be able to transfer their knowledge of how language works from the home language to their new language. Interaction with adults and peers is fundamental to language development in general and so it is important that the home language continues to be developed, at home and in school where possible and that new words learned in English are linked to the words already used in their home language.

Older pupils will come into school with different experiences of language use. Many pupils, particularly those whose families come from the Indian Sub-Continent, operate in a number of different languages, according to the context. Leung (2001) refers to a study of a Punjabi family in London whose members used Punjabi for social purposes, wrote and read poetry in Punjabi and Gurumukhi, read newspapers in Urdu, English and Hindi, and used Hindi to read the notices in the temple. Some pupils will be fluent in everyday English and some will be beginners; some will be literate in their home language but some will be developing literacy only in English. All additional language learners will have their different needs and we must not fall into the trap of assuming that because a pupil is fluent and confident in the language of the playground and everyday life that he or she is sufficiently fluent in the academic language needed to achieve well in school. Some new additional language learners will begin to try out words soon after arrival, some will remain silent until they are confident enough to speak. Both of these reactions are 'normal' but the pupils will need different means of support.

Research shows that additional language learning develops in same way regardless of the mother tongue of the learner and that some aspects of the new language are learned when the learner perceives a need and some can be learned in no particular sequence (Franson, 2009). Learners will go through some of the same stages of language acquisition as in a first language, see Table 2.1, for example the stage when a grammatical rule is generalized as in 'foot' becoming 'foots'. However, as with all learners the rate of development will depend upon the individual learner.

How pupils learn another language, and the strategies they employ, will necessarily change with age and experience. For young children, language development is taking place alongside their developing knowledge and understanding of the world around them. Older learners already have a wider experience of the world and bring with them the knowledge, understanding and skills from previous schooling. Their home language knowledge will help them to learn the additional language because they will be learning new ways to express ideas and concepts they are already familiar with. All languages share some common characteristics because all languages are governed by rules but the rules vary from language to language. Different languages use different ways of expressing concepts, applying grammatical rules in particular ways and using particular vocabulary. Part of the process of acquiring a new language is the discovery and application of these rules and this process often results in some confusion and the misapplication of rules of the home language to the new language. Franson (2009) calls the language that learners produce as they learn a new language 'Interlanguage' and points out that pupils will make mistakes as they learn but most errors in this 'Interlanguage' can be seen as a sign of progress and the internalizing of the way the new language works, for instance 'she goed' instead of 'went' is a generalization of the grammatical rule of forming the past tense.

What we know about additional language acquisition

There is a large body of well-substantiated research into second language acquisition (see Hall et al. 2001). The following features are generally recognized and are referred to in many local authority guidance materials:

- Pupils may take up to two years (some take longer) to develop social language, the language of the playground. This is what Cummins (1984) has called 'basic interpersonal communication skills' (BICS).
- It can take a further five to seven years for a pupil to acquire the range of literacy skills needed to cope well with GCSE subjects and beyond. Cummins called this 'cognitive, academic language proficiency' (CALP). See below for information about BICS and CALP.
- A silent (receptive) period in the early stages of learning an additional language is natural and should not be regarded as a sign of learning difficulties.
- Pupils will learn English in roughly the same way regardless of their first language background.
- Use of the first language is a valuable support to learning and not a hindrance. The use of both languages should be encouraged both at home and at school because literacy skills can be transferred from one language to another.
- Parents should be encouraged to share language and literacy in speaking and listening as well as reading and writing, both in their first language and in English. If their English is not good they should be encouraged to speak mainly in their first language in the home.
- One of the most powerful motivations for new language learning is the need to communicate in real situations, in this instance in the mainstream classroom.
- Bilingualism can be educationally enriching and have a positive effect on intellectual performance
- Additional language learners should never be regarded as having special educational needs simply because their home language is different.
- Where there are academic difficulties teachers should look first at their teaching approaches, in terms of motivation and use of language, before calling for SEN assessment.

(Adapted from Hall et al. (2001) and Swansea Ethnic Minority Language and Achievement Service, 2008)

BICS and CALP: moving from the concrete to the abstract

Basic Interpersonal Communication Skills (BICS) and Cognitive Academic Language Proficiency (CALP) are terms developed by Cummins (1984) to describe the process of learning an additional language. They are used frequently in literature and guidance materials for teachers of additional language learners. Cummins uses a simple two dimensional matrix to show how learning can be satisfactorily supported to enable pupils to move from the functional use of everyday language (BICS), which can take up to two years or longer, to proficiency in academic language (CALP), which may take up to seven further years to reach a stage comparable with first language English peers.

The horizontal axis of the matrix, see Figure 3.1, represents a continuum from 'context embedded' where there are lots of external clues such as gestures, pictures and real objects, to 'context reduced' where the learner relies upon text and knowledge of the language to make meaning. The vertical axis of the matrix is a continuum from cognitively undemanding, where tasks are simple and practical to cognitively demanding where tasks are more challenging. In principle tasks should progress from the lower left quadrant, where tasks are simple and there are plenty of contextual clues, to the upper right quadrant where tasks are challenging, there are few contextual clues beyond the task itself and where academic language is needed to cope with the cognitive demands.

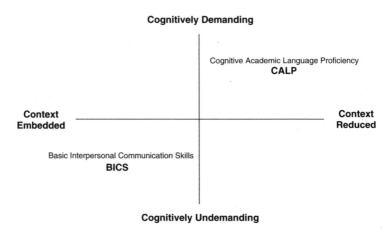

Figure 3.1 The Cummins Framework

The principle of gradually reducing contextual support and helping pupils to move from the concrete to the abstract in their learning is shown in the following diagram:

Concrete Primary Experiences	Contextualized Secondary Experiences	Two-dimensional Experiences	Abstract Situations
Multi-sensory	Multi-sensory	Single sense (usually seeing or hearing)	Symbols
Visits	Drama	Pictures	Discussion
Experimentation	Role play	Flash cards	Writing messages
	Models, toys	Cut outs	
	Videos	Diagrams	
		Maps	

Source: (Conteh and Brock, 2006:11)

We will return to the Cummins Framework in Chapter 8 to consider it as a model for planning, and further information and examples of the matrix in use can be found in Hall et al (2001).

A 'stress free' environment

Earlier in this chapter we said that first language learning normally takes place in a stress-free environment, so it seems sensible that if we wish pupils to learn an additional language, English, then we must try to make the school environment as stress free as possible. We know that language is intimately bound up with identity (see Chapter 2) and that when a child or a young person is surrounded by a new language and an unfamiliar environment then he or she is likely to feel insecure and anxious. The first step in learning the new language is to help the pupil to feel comfortable and supported and it is important that the school does what it can to create a stress-free environment by employing several very basic strategies:

- Ensure that all pupils feel safe and valued and know that they are protected from harassment, racial or otherwise.
- Ensure that staff become familiar, where possible, with the home language and with child's culture.
- Encourage pupils to take risks when speaking English but do not push them if they do not want to speak.
- Give pupils learning EAL opportunities to work alongside peers and adults who model English well.

- Emphasize that it is important that parents and pupils are encouraged to maintain and develop their home language because this provides a basis for the learning of English as an additional language.

(Adapted from DfES, 2002e)

These points will be expanded, with examples, in later chapters.

Writing systems

Pupils who are literate in their first language will have a general understanding of how language systems work, which should help them in their learning of written English. Leung (2001) tells us that literate pupils are likely to understand:

- that written language is a code which they can learn
- that written language is often different from spoken language in its vocabulary and expressions
- that there are rules for decoding (reading) and encoding (writing), such as spelling conventions and the sounds attributed to letters and letter groups
- that it may be necessary to interpret the meaning of a text and not take the words literally.

However, pupils whose linguistic backgrounds involve a system of writing which is different from that used in English may encounter a range of difficulties when learning how to read and write in English. Written English uses the Roman alphabet. Pupils whose first language uses an alphabetic system, even if it is not Roman, such as Russian or Greek, are likely to find it easier to learn to read and write in English than pupils whose first language uses a logographic (Chinese), consonantal (Arabic) or syllabic (Hindi) writing system. An awareness of different writing systems is useful for teachers of pupils who are literate in their first language so that they can recognize some of the common errors their pupils may make, for instance Bengali writing hangs from the line whereas English writing sits on it and Bengali script does not make a distinction between capital and lower case letters. Both of these rules of Bengali writing might be transferred to writing in English and could be seen, at least in the first instance, as examples of the 'Interlanguage' referred to above rather than real problems with grammar.

Some examples of different writing systems

The examples of the different scripts below are all translations of Article 8 of the United Nations Convention on the Rights of the Child:

Article 8

1. States Parties undertake to respect the right of the child to preserve his or her identity, including nationality, name and family relations as recognized by law without unlawful interference.

1. Alphabetic writing systems
• The Roman alphabet

Many languages, in Europe and in the wider world, use the Roman alphabet in their writing. Some of these languages such as German, French, Spanish and Turkish are familiar and we might be able to read them or at least recognize some words. Others, such as Croatian, Somali and Malay will be less familiar but we will recognize the letters used and we will be able to recognize patterns of words and sentences. We can also expect that the sounds of words will be represented by letters and combinations of letters.

Text in Malay (the Latin alphabet replaced Arabic in Malay writing in the seventeenth century)

Pasal 8

1. Negara-negara Pihak untuk menghormati hak anak untuk mempertahankan identiti dirinya, termasuk kebangsaan, nama dan hubungan keluarga seperti yang diakui oleh undang-undang tanpa melanggar undang-undang.

• The Cyrillic alphabet

Some languages such as Russian and Serbian, use the Cyrillic alphabetic system. The writing system works as with Roman alphabet but different symbols (letters) represent the different sounds.

Text in Russian

Статья 8

Все люди рождаются свободными и равными в своем достоинстве и правах. Они наделены разумом и совестью и должны поступать в отношении друг друга в духе братства

• The Greek alphabet

This alphabetic system also works like the Roman but uses different symbols for sounds. It is used in Greece and Cyprus.

Text in Greek

Άρθρο 8

1. Τα κρατικά συμβαλλόμενα μέρη αναλαμβάνουν να σεβαστούν το δικαίωμα του παιδιού να συντηρήσουν την ταυτότητά του/της,

συμπεριλαμβανομένης της υπηκοότητας, του ονόματος και των οικογενειακών σχέσεων όπως αναγνωρίζονται από το νόμο χωρίς παράνομη παρέμβαση.

2. Logographic writing systems

Some languages, such as Chinese, use characters to represent whole words or parts of words. Pupils who are literate in Chinese are likely to have more difficulty in learning to recognize the symbols and structures of words and sentences in English than pupils whose first language uses an alphabetic system. Traditionally Chinese characters were written in columns from right to left but since the middle of the twentieth century horizontal rows from left to right have become the norm.

Text in Chinese

第八条
1。缔约国承担尊重儿童维护其身份，包括国籍，姓名和家庭关系的法律承认，不进行非法干。

3. Consonantal writing systems

In a consonantal system the vowels are omitted from the writing, leaving the symbols for the consonant sounds. This causes little difficulty as 'wds cn b ndrstd qte wll n ths wy' but pupils used to this system may take time to understand that all letters in English words need to be written. Consonantal languages include Urdu, Arabic and Farsi and they are written from right to left, another factor to bear in mind when working with pupils who are literate in these languages.

Text in Arabic

المادة 18. وتتعهد الدول الأطراف باحترام حق الطفل في الحفاظ على هويته ، بما في ذلك جنسيته واسمه وصلاته العائلية على النحو الذي يقره القانون دون تدخل غير شرعي.

4. Syllabic writing systems

In syllabic systems the basic units of written language are syllables, usually a consonant and a vowel. The symbols convey these syllable units, for example 'da' or 'du'. Examples of syllabic languages are Hindi, Punjabi, Bengali, Gujarati and Tamil and they are written from left to right but the symbols hang from the line rather than sit upon it as in English.

Text in Hindi

अनुच्छेद 8
1. राज्यों दलों के लिए बच्चे का सही करने के लिए अपने या उसकी राष्ट्रीयता सहित पहचान, नाम और परिवार के साथ संबंधों के रूप में कानून द्वारा मान्यता प्राप्त सम्मान की रक्षा करने का कार्य

5. Mixed writing systems

Japanese is an example of a system which does not fit properly into any of the categories described above. It is a mixed system combining syllabic and logographic elements from traditional Japanese writing systems and from Chinese. More recently it has acquired some Roman letters, for example DVD. Traditionally, Japanese is written in columns going from top to bottom, with the columns ordered from right to left, as in traditional Chinese, but modern Japanese also uses a format which is more familiar to us: horizontal and reading from left to right.

Text in Japanese

第8条

1。締約国は、児童の権利を国籍を含む彼または彼女のアイデンティティを、名前や

家族の関係法律によって不法な干渉なしに認識保持を尊重することを約束。

Kenner (2004), in her book *Becoming Bi-literate: Young Children Learning Different Writing Systems*, has an interesting chapter on writing different scripts in which she describes primary school EAL learners, literate in their home languages, teaching their classmates to write some everyday words and phrases in their different languages. She describes the enjoyment of her pupils as they went about this activity and points out how the general language awareness developing in these young children will contribute to a far wider range of knowledge and understanding which can be applied across the curriculum. It has a part to play in any topic which involves looking at how people live, from knowledge of the local area and beyond in geography, to local and global citizenship and the similarities and differences between cultures and belief systems.

Key Points

- Effective communication involves more than learning words and there are several important processes involved in the effective use of language for communication.
- There is a recognized sequence of first language development in babies and children. Additional language development shares some, but not all, of these developmental stages.
- Errors in grammar, in speech and writing, often denote 'Interlanguage' where the rules of the first language are applied to the new language. This is part of the process of acquiring a new language.
- There is a large body of readily available knowledge about additional language acquisition.

Moving on: some suggestions for further enquiry

- Investigate the website of the National Association for Language Development in the Curriculum (NALDIC) http://www.naldic.org.uk/ to find recent research papers on aspects of additional language acquisition which interest you or help to answer some of your questions.
- Investigate different writing systems and the errors they prompt in pupils learning to write English. See: Kenner, C. (2004) *Becoming Bi-literate: Young Children Learning Different Writing Systems.* Stoke on Trent: Trentham Books. Go to http://www.omniglot.com for a range of information about different languages and how they are written.

Further reading

Baker, C. and Hornberger, N. (eds.) (2001) *An Introductory Reader to the Writings of Jim Cummins.* Clevedon: Multilingual Matters

Berko-Gleason, J. (2001) *The Development of Language. Fifth Edition.* London: Allyn and Bacon

Crystal, D. (2007) *How Language Works: How Babies Babble, Words Change Meaning and Languages Live or Die.* Harmondsworth: Penguin Books

Foster-Cohen, S. (1999) *An Introduction to Child Language Development.* London: Longman

McLeod, S. (2007) *The International Guide to Speech Acquisition.* London: Thomson Learning Inc.

Sheridan, M.D. (1997) *From Birth to Five Years.* London: Routledge

A Language Rich Environment

4

This chapter will focus on the importance of a learning environment which is rich in opportunities for practising and developing language, particularly spoken language. Sections will include:

pedagogy
collaborative talk
drama
language across the curriculum
questioning

The standards for qualified teacher status addressed will be those relating to teaching and learning including the following which refer to skill development:

QTS standards for England

Q15 Know and understand the relevant statutory and non-statutory curricula and frameworks, including those provided through the National Strategies, for their subjects/curriculum areas, and other relevant initiatives

Q23 Design opportunities for learners to develop their literacy, numeracy and ICT skills.

QTS standards for Wales

S2.1 (b) for Key Stage 2, that they:

(iii) know and understand the most recent national guidance on developing thinking, communication, ICT and number skills, for example that set out in the *Skills Framework for 3 to 19-year-olds in Wales*; and

(c) for Key Stage 3, that:

(i) they know and understand the relevant National Curriculum Programme(s) of Study and the most recent national guidance on developing thinking, communication, ICT and number skills, for example that set out in the *Skills Framework for 3 to 19-year-olds in Wales*; and

(ii) if they are qualifying to teach one or more of the core subjects, they are familiar with the principles of *Aiming for Excellence in Key Stage 3* and with the subsequent guidance materials *Raising Standards in Literacy and Numeracy*; *Raising Standards in Information and Communication Technology*; and *Raising Standards: Transition from Key Stage 2 to Key Stage 3*.

Reflection

Think about a lesson you have recently taught. What opportunities did pupils have to talk to each other as part of the lesson? How much consideration did you give to the questions you asked them, particularly in the introduction and in the plenary at the end of the lesson?

Pedagogy

First a word about teaching in general: a firm understanding of pedagogy, the art or maybe the science of teaching, requires a good understanding of the nature of the learning process and the ways in which children and young people learn. A good grasp of basic pedagogical principles, including the central importance of language, enables teachers to tailor their teaching to the needs of individuals and groups of pupils, including additional language learners. In general the teaching methods and approaches which have been developed for mixed ability teaching have been shown to work well with EAL pupils: inclusive methods, employing collaboration and talk and using approaches and resources which reflect diversity in gender, culture and learning styles. These methods are also the basis for teaching PSE and citizenship so it is important as well as useful for teachers to develop a repertoire of transferable strategies which involve active learning, where pupils are encouraged to participate and collaborate, and where they are given the opportunity to discuss and reflect upon their learning. Books and materials for use in PSE and citizenship lessons are good sources of ideas for appropriate activities which can be used in different curriculum areas and some are given at the end of the chapter.

Collaborative talk

Good speaking and listening skills and the opportunity to develop and employ them are important for all pupils in order to make sense of experiences and to develop their understanding of ideas and concepts. Hall et al (2001:4) tell us that:

> Pupils who engage orally in the language of a subject with their peers are more likely to understand and internalize related concepts.

Planned talk with a partner or in a group gives pupils the opportunity to practise a range of thinking and language skills and to develop some of the social skills necessary to work successfully with other people. Apart from providing the opportunity to hone speaking and listening skills, carefully planned group talk can stimulate higher order thinking such as predicting, hypothesis testing, evaluating and justifying, and can encourage metacognitive processes such as reflecting on how the group reached its conclusion or answer.

The richness of learning presented by group talk, in terms of the contribution to language development, thinking and social development, has implications for teachers' planning. In fact it is strongly recommended, by the DfES among others, that speaking and listening activities should be planned, where possible before any writing activities. The quality of all pupils' writing, not only EAL learners, will benefit from the extended language and thinking involved. In a later chapter we will consider the use of frames to support speaking for different purposes, similar to writing frames for different genres of writing.

Conteh et al (2006) emphasize the importance of spoken language to underpin writing. They suggest a method which they call 'rich scripting' as a way in which new language can be used in different contexts moving from context rich to increasingly context reduced, applying the model presented in the Cummins Framework (see Chapter 3). They suggest a three stage process of introducing and using new words which helps pupils to develop a deeper understanding than using simplified vocabulary or giving them lists of definitions.

> Stage 1: Talk about things in the 'here and now' using real objects, 'hands on' experience and introducing the new vocabulary. (context embedded)
>
> Stage 2: Talk about what they have done, not immediately connected with what they are doing now (report or recount), and rehearsing the new vocabulary. (reducing the context)
>
> Stage 3: Talk or write about what they have done in a more formal or academic way using the new vocabulary. (moving along the cognitive dimension of Cummins' framework while still retaining contextual scaffolding)

It can be a problem to convince pupils that talking is an important part of learning as many may be under the impression that only writing is 'work'. Robin Alexander has written extensively about the importance of talk to learning and he points out that in British schools 'considerably lower educational status is ascribed to talk than to writing, and this difference is constantly reinforced' (Alexander 2005:9). He suggests that we should pay more attention to the place of talk in children's learning and development, and not place so much importance on writing as evidence of learning.

Just as it is important to train pupils to work effectively in groups, so it is important to develop the kind of classroom culture that will allow and support collaborative talk. Essentially this will be an ethos which promotes respect for all members of the class. Working with pupils to discuss and develop guidelines for group work and talk can be a very productive way forward. Wells and Chang-Wells (1992, in Conteh et al 2006:45) suggest guidelines for teachers on how to develop a classroom ethos which will promote collaborative talk. Their suggestions focus on how the teacher relates to pupils and they stress the importance of the teacher demonstrating a serious and respectful attitude' towards pupils. They suggest that the teacher guidelines could also be used as a basis for agreeing class guidelines:

- Always take seriously what pupils say.
- Listen carefully to what they say and ask questions to make sure you fully understand the points they want to make.
- When you respond try to extend and develop what children say and encourage them to do this themselves.
- Try to take account of what you know about the individual pupil, treating each pupil as a serious conversation partner.
- While keeping learning objectives in mind try to modify your responses in the light of what pupils say.

Drama/role play

The use of drama techniques is a valuable way of promoting language in the classroom and can be used across the curriculum. Fellowes (2006:75) gives a number of reasons why drama can be such an important teaching and learning strategy:

- It extends pupils' language by allowing the teacher to have opportunities to introduce and model new language and by giving pupils the opportunity to use this language in a natural and active way.
- It enables pupils to talk for a range of different purposes and therefore to adapt their language to fit the situation.
- It promotes thinking and learning through talk and can give pupils the opportunity to practise skills such as explaining, hypothesizing, negotiating.
- It promotes listening as well as talk.
- It encourages the development of social skills such as cooperation and empathy
- It provides the stimulus for writing of various kinds including creative writing.

There is a wide range of different drama techniques, most of which are not difficult to organize. Some of these, such as hot seating and teacher in role are well known but others such as forum theatre, freeze frames and conscience alley are less so. Role cards and prompt cards for role plays and debates can be found in teaching materials for many curriculum areas and are not difficult to adapt to the needs of particular pupils. Some suggestions for further reading on drama techniques can be found at the end of the chapter and PSE and citizenship materials, referred to above, are a good source of resources and ideas for role plays, debates and other drama activities.

Drama activities are not difficult to organize in the classroom but they do need to be well planned and appropriately resourced. Fellowes (2006:86) gives the following list of principles for successful drama work:

- successful drama activities need a strong and explicit structure
- 'good' literature provides powerful stories and a memorable text on which to base drama activities
- pupils need time to absorb what is being asked of them and develop ideas to contribute to the drama
- take part in the drama as much as possible – share the learning experiences with your pupils
- set up a conflict – a situation where pupils (in role) need to oppose a story or forceful character
- build bilingualism into the activity as much as possible, providing opportunities for pupils to use their first language in role
- involve as many pupils as possible for short periods.

Language across the curriculum

We know from Chapter 3 that EAL pupils take longer to become proficient in academic language than social language. Many first language English pupils also struggle with particular genres of writing and the specialized vocabulary needed in different curriculum areas, so the idea of the language rich environment needs to be applied across the curriculum to ensure that all pupils can develop the range of language and writing styles they need. All teachers are teachers of language as well as teachers of their subject specialisms and need to be aware of the kinds of language used in the texts their pupils are working with, in their reading and their writing.

Walters (2007:160) suggests the following points to bear in mind when reading with the class:

- Give the purpose of the reading before the students read.
- Activate the students' prior knowledge – find out what they know already about the topic.
- Direct them to particular features of the text: build awareness.
- Model reading (think aloud).
- Allow uninterrupted time for reading.

- Think of a way of covering what has been read so that beginner EAL pupils can stay part of the lesson.

The support booklets provided by the DfES for the Key Stage 3 National Strategy, for example DfES (2002d) below, set out some excellent examples of language support strategies for each curriculum area, including the use of writing frames and grids to support writing, and although they are intended for EAL support the activities and strategies suggested are appropriate for all pupils and can be modified for use in Key Stage 2.

Science as an example

The examples which follow come from *Access and Engagement in Science: Teaching Pupils for Whom English is an Additional Language* (DfES 2002d) but the principles are transferable to other curriculum areas, as are those described in the other booklets in the series. The section on 'Improving Scientific Literacy' begins by referring to the findings of the Ofsted secondary report 2000/1 where it was noted that many science departments were paying extra attention to language in their lessons. Particular strategies were seen as being particularly supportive:

- reinforcement of meanings and use of terminology in context rather than simply providing lists of definitions
- reduction in routine written descriptions of practical activity and more writing about pupils' own understanding and interpretation of information
- extending writing for other purposes such as recording and discussion of 'ideas' and 'evidence'
- reading about science issues as well as reading for information.

Scientific terminology

It is important that when pupils are speaking and writing about science they use scientific terms precisely and this is not always straightforward. Most science departments produce vocabulary lists but some of these contain too many words and the words may be out of context. The careful introduction of small numbers of words, to be used in the context of a particular topic, is more manageable and better for learning. Classifying words according to their function has also been shown to be useful, for example:

- **Naming** words: cell, cytoplasm, hydrogen.
- **Process** words: diffusion, digestion.
- **Concept** words: magnetism, particles.

It is also helpful to put words in alphabetical order and to identify any words which have difficult meanings or spellings. New words should then be used in the lesson, modelled by the teacher and built into shared talking activity so that they can be used in talk before they need to be used in written work.

Some words cause confusion for other reasons:

- Many words used in science also have an 'everyday' meaning, e.g. cell, force and time. These words can cause confusion for many pupils but particularly additional language learners and time will need to be devoted to developing understanding of the meanings of these words in different contexts.
- Some words are easy to read but difficult to understand, e.g. atom, energy. Developing understanding will require explanation, exemplification and time to use the words in meaningful talk.
- Some words may be misspelled because the Latin and Greek roots of words are not known and patterns of words sharing the same roots are not recognized, for example 'photosynthesis' may be spelled 'photosinthesus' because the connection with the word 'synthesis' is not made. The booklet gives a useful example of how pupils can be supported by learning the root meanings of the scientific words they need to use.

Use of personalized dictionaries in Year 7 Science

Pupils were encouraged to use personalized dictionaries with a section for roots and meanings. Teachers took time in most lessons to break down and explain the meanings of words with Greek or Latin roots. For example:

Root	Meaning
Chlor-	Green
Poly-	Many
Therm-	Heat
Hydro-	Water
Electro-	Electricity
Photo-	Light
-ose	carbohydrate
-lys	breakdown

Pupils were then encouraged to look for the roots in new words and to identify groups of words which shared the same roots – a fruitful focus for discussion and shared talk. (Adapted from DfES 2002d:11)

Questioning

Teacher questions

Questioning is an essential part of teaching and learning, for teachers and for pupils, and is the stimulus for most of the talk in classrooms. Good questioning skills are essential to promote good thinking and therefore good learning (we will return to this in Chapter 8) but Wragg and Brown (2001:28) suggest that there are common errors in teachers' questioning techniques that it would be well to address:

Common 'errors' in questioning

- Asking too many questions at once.
- Asking a question and answering it yourself.
- Asking questions only of the brightest or most likeable pupils.
- Asking a difficult question too early in the sequence of events.
- Asking irrelevant questions.
- Always asking the same type of questions (e.g. closed ones).
- Asking questions in a threatening way.
- Not using probing questions.
- Not giving pupils time to think.
- Not correcting wrong answers.
- Ignoring pupils' answers.
- Failing to see the implications of pupils' answers.
- Failing to build on answers.

The Key Stage 3 National Strategy (DfES 2003, p.6) gives a useful list of the questioning skills that classroom practitioners need to develop:

Common teaching skills: questioning

- Questions need to be planned in a sequence that guides pupils towards and reinforces the main objectives of the lesson
- Certain types of question have inbuilt challenge and require pupils to think deeply:
  - open-ended questions that have no one obvious answer;
  - questions that demand and develop higher-order thinking skills such as analysis, synthesis and evaluation;
  - questions that encourage pupils to speculate and take risks.
- Teachers should build in 'wait time' so that pupils can reflect on a challenging question before answering it.

- Questions can be used to promote active listening and engagement, especially when the 'no hands up' rule is used. Active listening skills can be developed further by building variety into a teacher's questions and expecting pupils to generate their own questions.
- Teachers can encourage pupils to give extended answers using questions and other strategies, such as inviting pupils to elaborate or speculate on a topic.

Pupil questions

It is obviously important for teachers to develop their questioning skills as part of their professional repertoire but it is also important for pupils to develop their own questioning skills. Encouraging pupils to generate their own questions for enquiry and research is a way of actively involving pupils in their own learning and providing a genuine stimulus for talk. A simple strategy which has been used successfully in many classrooms in Key Stage 2 and Key Stage 3 is the use of frameworks to support questioning, such as KWL grids (What do I Know? What do I Want to Know? What have I Learned?) and variations such as KWH (What do I Know? What do I Want to Know? How Will I Find Out?)

The example which follows is part of a grid used in a Year 6 class in a topic on Victorians. The pupils worked in pairs to summarize the information they had already collected and to devise questions for further enquiry. The grid was used enthusiastically by pupils who engaged in productive discussion and generated some useful questions. This particular example has prompts in Turkish to support a recently arrived Turkish speaking pupil.

Victorian Zamanindaki Çocuklar 1837–1901 Evler Children in the Victorian Period 1837–1901 Focus: Homes		
Ne biliriz? **What do we Know?**	**Ne bilmek isteriz?** **What do we Want to Know?**	**Nasil bulabiliriz?** **How Will we Find Out?**
Town Country Living conditions (heating, lighting, washing)		

Planning

Providing a language-rich environment for all pupils has implications for planning in both Key Stage 2 and Key Stage 3. It needs an awareness of the language requirements of different curriculum areas, the writing genres and specialized vocabulary, and a recognition of the opportunities afforded by different activities in different curriculum areas. If we accept that language is central to learning and if we think in terms of 'it's not just what you do, it's the way that you do it' then it becomes possible to plan for the curriculum and for the language development of all pupils, not only the EAL learners. A simple way to start is by always building in a focused talking activity, especially before any writing activity.

Conteh and Brock (2006:9 in Conteh 2006) set out some key principles for planning and organizing learning activities for additional language learners which particularly emphasize the importance of first language and talk and although they are presented in the context of Key stage 2, they are equally applicable to Key Stage 3.

Principles for planning activities

- Support in the first language and opportunities to use it for themselves in different ways in their everyday classroom activities will open out potential for learning in bilingual pupils.
- Promoting home languages in school is an important way to support home-school links, and encourages families and schools to work in partnership.
- Talk is one of the most important channels and tools for learning; pupils construct their knowledge in the classroom in all subjects through talk and so need every possible opportunity to explore ideas and concepts through talk, not just in English and in the Literacy Hour.
- The best writing develops from powerful and meaningful experiences, usually mediated by talk – before beginning extended writing activities, pupils always need the chance for collaborative discussion and planning.
- Knowledge of more than one language promotes awareness of language systems and structures; this awareness needs to be supported and can be used as a valuable teaching and learning tool.
- All learning, and especially language learning, is enhanced and strengthened by opportunities for hands-on experience.

EAL and additional learning difficulties

General language difficulties

A child will usually develop social language, i.e. be able to chat with friends within about two years, though it will take much longer to become proficient in the academic language needed for examination purposes. If a pupil has a persisting difficulty acquiring a new language, despite a language-rich environment and a generally supportive learning environment it may be that there is an underlying problem with language acquisition. In this case a speech and language therapist may be needed to make an accurate assessment and plan a programme of support.

Attention deficit

It can be difficult for pupils to concentrate and stay focused when working in a new language. Particularly in the early stages of learning English pupils may need to take 'time out' and may look as if they are bored or being deliberately inattentive. Attention and listening should improve as language competency develops but it is important that the difficulties in attention due to new language acquisition do not mask any underlying attention problem where specific help may be needed.

Key Points

- Language is central to learning; therefore a language rich environment is important for all pupils.
- Inclusive teaching methods, developed for mixed ability teaching, are appropriate for EAL pupils.
- It is important to provide plenty of opportunities for talk, including focused collaborative talk, drama and rehearsal of specialized vocabulary.
- Talk is important as a support for writing.

Moving on: suggestions for further enquiry

- If you are working in Key stage 3 find the guidance booklet for your curriculum area. http://nationalstrategies.standards.dcsf.gov.uk/search/inclusion/results/nav:50106
- Find time to do a language-focused observation of a pupil, an additional language pupil if possible. Look at how the pupil:
  - Works with others, as a partner or in a group: does s/he ask and answer direct questions; copy behaviours and expressions; collaborate on a task; lead a group activity; look to another pupil for guidance?

- uses language in different contexts: in the playground; talking one-to-one with an adult; talking with peers in the classroom; in a whole class situation.

Further reading

Conteh, J. (ed.) (2006) *Promoting Learning for Bilingual Pupils 3–11.* London: Sage Publications

Wragg, E.C. and Brown, G. (2001) *Questioning in the Primary School.* London: RoutledgeFalmer

Wragg, E.C. and Brown, G. (2001) *Questioning in the Secondary School.* London: RoutledgeFalmer

PSE/Citizenship

Claire, H. (ed.) (2004) *Teaching Citizenship in Primary Schools.* Exeter: Learning Matters

Claire H. (2001) Not Aliens: Primary School Children and the Citizenship/PSHE Curriculum. Stoke on Trent: Trentham Books

Clough N, and Holden, C. (2002) *Education for Citizenship: Ideas into Action.* London: RoutledgeFalmer

Eaude, T. (2006) *Children's Spiritual, Moral, Social and Cultural Development.* Exeter: Learning Matters

Drama techniques

Ashcroft, J. and Pearce, L. (1996) Drama Activities for Key Stage 3. Dunstable: Folens

Fellowes, A. (2001) *Bilingual Shakespeare: A Practical Approach for Teachers.* Stoke on Trent: Trentham Books

Neelands, J. (1984) *Making Sense of Drama: A Guide to Classroom Practice.* Oxford: Heinemann Educational Books

Prendiville, F. and Toye, N. (2007) Speaking and Listening Through Drama, 7–11. London: Paul Chapman

5 The Supportive Learning Environment

A supportive learning environment is essential for all learners but there are several elements of such an environment which need to be given special consideration for additional language learners. This chapter will focus on the following aspects of classroom and school life which are particularly important here:

- information about pupils and families
- culture and religion
- the importance of valuing the individual
- resources including support staff
- specialist language support staff
- use of first language
- pupil grouping and collaborative practice
- subject teaching in secondary schools
- welcoming new pupils

The topics in the chapter will be relevant to a number of standards for QTS which apply not only to EAL learners but to learners in general. Those set out here at the beginning are the ones which explicitly focus on the learning environment but other standards statements will be found in later sections of the chapter.

QTS standard for England

Q 30 Establish a purposeful and safe learning environment conducive to learning and identify opportunities for learners to learn in out-of-school contexts.

QTS standard for Wales

S3.3.1 They have high expectations of learners and build successful relationships, centred on teaching and learning. They establish a purposeful learning environment where diversity is valued and where learners feel secure and confident.

Reflection

Think about your classroom, or the one you have been in most recently. What aspects of classroom life and practise can you identify as being supportive to all the learners in the class?

Establishing a supportive learning environment

All learners learn best in an environment which is comfortable and pleasant and in which they feel safe. Classrooms are where much of the learning in school takes place, and they are the area of a school where an individual teacher can really make a difference; communal areas such as playgrounds, dining rooms and corridors require much more of a collective effort. A good understanding of the background conditions for successful learning and good classroom management skills are needed in order to provide a supportive learning environment for all learners. A supportive learning environment for EAL learners, goes beyond the basics of classroom management: time, space and resource management and pupil organisation, although these are all important. It also involves more than the atmosphere or 'culture' of the classroom.

QTS standard for England

Q 18 Understand how children and young people develop and that the progress and well-being of learners are affected by a range of developmental, social, religious, ethnic, cultural and linguistic influences.

QTS standard for Wales

S2.4 They understand how learners' physical, intellectual, linguistic, social, cultural and emotional development can affect their learning.

Information about pupils and families

The first contact between parents, pupil and the school should, of course, be friendly and positive. In a perfect world the school should be welcoming, interpretation and translation services should be available and there should be appropriate information about the family and the pupil. This is not always possible, however, and very often families arrive at school with little warning and support.

Information about the pupil's background and family, where this is available, should be accessible to all teachers and TAs involved because family circumstances play an important part in how a pupil settles into school and in their attitude and motivation to learn a new language. A clear example of a background which might interfere with both learning and behaviour is a child or a young person of an asylum seeking family who might have suffered traumatic experiences as the family left their home and travelled to the United Kingdom. In this instance a teacher would need to be particularly sensitive and supportive to both pupil and family. Refugee families will not have chosen freely to leave their home and some may be frightened and suspicious of people asking personal questions. Some schools are fortunate enough to have a specialist member of staff and the facilities to deal with children traumatized by violence and war.

An important piece of family information which will be assessed in an early interview by specialist staff is the extent of parents' literacy in English and in their home language. Parental literacy has a marked influence upon the development of language and literacy in their children.

Pupils who join a school in Key Stage 2 or 3 will usually have been to school before, either in another part of the United Kingdom, possibly as a temporary resident, or in their home country. Their school records may or may not be available but it is important to try to find out what their previous school experience has been. The basic school syllabuses in many other countries cover the same content range and many countries have a National Curriculum broadly similar to that of England and Wales. Pupils will have some understanding of the curriculum content and possibly a better understanding than their new peers of some areas which have been given greater prominence in their previous schooling. Above all it is important to remember that all these pupils are bringing knowledge and skills with them and it is the English language which is new to them.

As a student or a new teacher there is little you can do about new admissions but there are some simple steps you can take to make new pupils feel welcome and supported. A smile is simple but important, as is learning the correct pronunciation of a pupil's name. The correct pronunciation and spelling of a name is very important to a person's self esteem, as anyone whose name is regularly mispronounced or misspelled will verify. Sitting with another speaker of the same language is a simple and obvious supportive strategy or if there is no other same language speaker you could appoint a classroom friend or buddy. There are also simple strategies you can use to help with classroom routines (see Chapter 7). The important factor here is to help the pupil feel as comfortable and safe as possible.

Culture and religion

The home culture of pupils is an important part of their identity, as we have already discussed. We may have pupils in our classes who come from a variety of religious backgrounds and not all of them will be additional language learners. It is important that teachers are aware of the basic tenets of the faiths to which their pupils belong and the dates of important events and festivals. Lack of awareness may result in misunderstanding a pupil's behaviour or responses and may cause offence to families and distress to pupils.

Teachers and support staff also need to be aware that different communities have different ideas of family life and the roles and responsibilities of family members. Codes of conduct may differ from those of the majority of staff and pupils and may appear unacceptable on both sides; so open communication between school, home and community is very important.

Case Study: how one primary school addresses some religious and cultural issues

This is a medium sized inner city primary school with Christian, Jewish and Muslim pupils on roll. The head teacher and staff have worked hard to develop good relationships with the local faith communities and their leaders.

- The school prayer, which is featured in several prominent places in the school, was written in consultation with the local Christian, Jewish and Muslim communities
- After some disquiet about the disciplinary strategies used by some teachers in the local mosque the head teacher offered in service training sessions to share school discipline practice. This allowed discussion about the relationship between Sharia law, regarding discipline, and the United Nations Convention on the Rights of the Child to which the school is deeply committed.
- The school serves a large Bangladeshi community, and extended holidays to visit relatives are a regular occurrence. The importance of family and cultural connections is recognized but the teachers are concerned about the impact on pupils' learning. With this in mind, the school has made an information video for parents explaining the implications of prolonged absence from school and the class-teacher makes up a holiday pack of work for pupils to take with them. There is a permanent language support teacher on the staff and she arranges 'catch up' lessons for pupils on their return.
- Family learning groups and ICT lessons have been organized, despite difficulties with some members of the local Bangladeshi community about empowering women – most people attending the sessions are mothers with children in the school. The problems were sorted out with the help and support from leaders of the local mosque and the groups and lessons are now well attended.

Valuing the individual

Providing opportunities for all pupils to share aspects of their out of school and home life is fundamental to valuing them as individuals. The relationship between language and identity was explored in Chapter 2 and we have already noted the importance of correct pronunciation of pupils' names, whether they be additional language learners or not. Finding out what languages our EAL learners use is important for us as teachers in order to help us to plan appropriately, but it is also important to pupils as recognition of the skills and experiences they are bringing with them into the classroom. Pupils can be encouraged to use their spoken and written languages to extend the general language awareness of their classmates. Kenner (2004) describes a project where six-year-old bi-lingual pupils 'taught' their classmates how to write in Arabic, Spanish or Chinese through carefully structured, peer-teaching sessions, arranged on a one-to-one basis in a quiet room.

> With the help of each school's primary school teacher, a quiet place for peer teaching was found, ranging from the school library to the staff room. There was no shortage of volunteer pupils – many children wanted to be the first to learn how to write in Chinese, Arabic or Spanish. Some even asked for homework and brought it back for inspection. (Kenner 2004:33)

Resources

QTS standard for England

> Q19 Know how to make effective personalized provision for those they teach, including those for whom English is an additional language or who have special educational needs or disabilities, and how to take practical account of diversity and promote equality and inclusion in their teaching.

QTS standard for Wales

> S3.1.3 They select and prepare resources, and plan for their safe and effective organization, taking account of learners' interests and their language and cultural backgrounds, with the help of support staff where appropriate.

Learning to choose and share resources is an important part of becoming an autonomous learner. Dual language texts and bilingual dictionaries and word lists are essential resources and pupils need to be able to access them easily. This is usually straightforward in primary classrooms where there are classroom-based libraries and resources, and pupils usually know where to find what they need. However, the situation in secondary classrooms might be very different where reference materials, like bilingual dictionaries, are held outside the classroom in the school library. Thought needs to be given to encouraging and making it easy for pupils to consult dictionaries and other support materials, both inside and outside the classroom.

Dictionaries and word lists are important not only for pupils but for teachers. Most teachers find that they have to make some of their own resources, particularly visual and specialized vocabulary resources. For EAL learners personalized resources such as vocabulary lists, illustrated word banks, picture and word matching activities, charts and diagrams (see Chapters 7 and 8) are an essential support to learning and the teacher or TA who is designing and making the resource will, in the main, rely upon a bilingual dictionary or vocabulary book.

Human resources

QTS standards for England

Q6 Have a commitment to collaboration and co-operative working.

Q20 Know and understand the roles of colleagues with specific responsibilities, including those with responsibility for learners with special educational needs and disabilities and other individual learning needs.

Q33 Ensure that colleagues working with them are appropriately involved in supporting learning and understand the roles they are expected to fulfil.

QTS standards for Wales

S1.6 They recognize and understand the contribution provided by and needed from support staff and other professionals in the learning process.

3.3.13 They work collaboratively with specialist teachers and other colleagues and, with the help of an experienced teacher as appropriate, manage the work of teaching assistants or other adults to enhance the learning of those they teach.

We know from the work of Piaget, Bruner and others that we build up our knowledge and understanding through interactions with our environment and with other people. In the classroom situation these interactions will be with peers or with adults, usually a teacher, teaching assistant (TA) or specialist member of staff. Language acquisition necessarily requires good quality speaking and listening opportunities which means that when we are considering additional language learners we need to take account of all the human resources at our disposal. We will consider pupil grouping and peer support later but here we need to take into account teaching assistants and other staff who can give classroom-based support both to pupils and to teachers.

Teaching assistants

Many classrooms now have at least one teaching assistant working with the teacher. Effective use of the teaching assistant can make an enormous contribution to the quality of learning of all pupils, not only the special educational needs pupils. An experienced and knowledgeable TA can support and encourage interaction, and therefore the quality of learning, in a variety of situations: on a one-to-one basis with an individual pupil, with a pair or small group and when working alongside the teacher with the whole class. It is important to remember, however, that learning English as an additional language is not in itself a learning difficulty and that it is not appropriate for a TA to provide one-to-one support in the same way as for a pupil with learning or speech and language difficulties.

A TA will also be able to help the teacher to produce specialized resources, either by making them from scratch using photographs, pictures and word lists collected for the purpose, or by adapting published resources.

To ensure that a TA is able to make a really effective contribution to learning it is necessary to find time for joint planning or at least for sharing lesson plans. This will not only let the TA know the learning intentions for lessons in time to prepare any necessary materials but will allow him or her to offer suggestions in the light of their knowledge of particular pupils, which may be better than the teacher's. Lesson plans, especially those of students and new teachers, should indicate the roles of TAs and other adults in the classroom.

Bilingual teaching assistants

Some schools will be fortunate to have the services of bilingual teaching assistants (BTAs) who are often professional people, qualified in other fields, who have chosen to work in this support capacity in schools. They are usually attached to the local Ethnic Minority Achievement Service and may be qualified as interpreters for admission appeals, statutory SEN assessments and other situations in education which have legal requirements. The role of BTAs in the classroom is to help pupils to access the curriculum through their home language and to continue to develop their home language while they are acquiring English.

The Swansea Ethnic Minority Language and Achievement Service (EMLAS) gives the following advice to schools about the use of BTAs which will be useful for students and new teachers to bear in mind if they have not worked in a classroom with a BTA before:

A bilingual support session will be most effective when:

- The BTA works in the classroom in a group setting.
- Lesson/topic plans are shared with the BTA in advance.
- Whole class teaching is kept to a minimum.
- Pupils' prior learning in and through their home language is activated and developed to help access on-going class work.

A bilingual support session will be least effective when:

- The is no liaison time between the BTA and school staff.
- The support is not linked to on-going class work.
- The teacher leads the whole class for most of the time.
- The BTA is used solely to listen to pupils reading.

Just as it is essential to share planning with the resident TA it is also important to share planning with the BTA so that he or she knows the curriculum aims of the session. The BTA can be asked to support in a variety of ways including translating, orally or in writing, pre-teaching key words and phrases related to the curriculum subject, supporting group discussions and translating captions and labels.

Specialist language support teachers

Language support teams have different titles in different places but their purpose is to support ethnic minority and other pupils who are learning English as an additional language. They provide specialist advice and support to schools and to pupils and play an important part in assessing the needs of EAL pupils and providing training and support materials for staff. Some schools with large numbers of EAL pupils have permanently attached specialist staff but this is unlikely to be the case in the many schools with just a handful of EAL pupils.

At the heart of the relationship between teachers, TAs and specialist staff is the principle of partnership teaching referred to in Chapter 1.

- Language support teachers work in partnership with class and subject teachers, planning curriculum delivery together to enhance the access of pupils learning EAL to subject knowledge, as well as developing their acquisition of the English language. Partnership teaching has helped class and subject teachers plan inclusively for pupils' learning without relying on the presence of a support teacher. This approach works well in schools where time is available for joint planning. It requires language support teachers to develop their subject knowledge, especially at secondary level.
- Language specialist and mainstream teachers plan the inclusive curriculum together. TAs support implementation in the classroom. TAs need to feel confident in supporting pupils' English language acquisition and curriculum learning. They need to be deployed effectively, with full access to lesson plans. (DfES 2002e:7)

Use of first language

We have seen in Chapter 3 that facility in a first language will help additional language acquisition, rather than hinder it. EAL pupils arriving in Key Stage 2 and 3 classrooms will be competent speakers of their first language and many will also be literate and able to communicate well in writing. The language and literacy skills of these pupils need to be acknowledged and used for learning and it is always important for teachers to remember that these pupils are not only learning English but also learning the curriculum content. The importance of talk cannot be overemphasized and talking with other pupils or bi-lingual teaching assistants sharing the first language, where this is possible, will help to clarify thinking and understanding of the subject matter. Writing in first language before writing in English will also help pupils to organize their thoughts and to be reflective, an important aspect of becoming an effective learner.

Gibbons (1991, in Conteh 2006:64) reminds us of three important aspects of learning: cognitive, affective and social, and suggests that encouraging pupils to use their full range of language skills i.e. speaking, reading and writing in their first language as well as in English, addresses all of these aspects. She outlines the advantages to pupils of using their first language for learning:

- It makes it easier for pupils to develop understanding of basic concepts by allowing them to draw on their total language experience.
- It helps to develop pupils' self confidence and self-esteem.

- It takes advantage of one of the greatest resources children bring to school, and is based on sound pedagogic principles.

Pupil grouping

QTS standard for England

Q25 (d) demonstrate the ability to manage the learning of individuals, groups and whole classes, modifying their teaching to suit the stage of the lesson.

Effective learning requires opportunities for interaction with others, adults and peers, in order to talk, question and reflect. For EAL pupils it is important to provide good models of spoken English and to provide opportunities for them to speak to adults and peers. Careful planning for speaking and listening is necessary both to allow them to learn English and to access the curriculum and this includes attention to pupil grouping.

When we group our pupils for learning we should be trying to provide them with opportunities for good quality interactions that will develop their skills and understanding but how best to organize them requires careful thought. Will the pupils learn best as a whole class, as individuals, in pairs or in groups? Who should be paired with whom or how should the groups be made up? Where do our EAL pupils fit in? The important point here is one of overarching importance: fitness for purpose. How to organize pupils for learning is the professional decision of the teacher, based on their knowledge of the pupils in the class and what they want the pupils to learn. Considerations for EAL pupils will be:

- Are there other pupils who speak the same language and can they work together? Should they always work together?
- Are there English speaking pupils in the class who could work with and provide a good model of language for the EAL pupil?
- Can pupils be organized to work in different groups at different times in order to encourage better understanding and social cohesion?

Collaborative practice

QTS standard for Wales

S3.3.3 They teach clearly structured lessons or sequences of work which interest and motivate learners and which
(b) employ interactive teaching methods and collaborative group work.

Collaborative work, in pairs or small groups, helps pupils to develop their thinking through talk, allows them to give and receive support and, if the work is carefully structured, allows each pupil to contribute and to achieve. It plays an important part in developing a classroom culture which promotes inclusion. Designing collaborative group work requires careful attention to the processes and procedures of the task as well as to the content, and planning to include EAL pupils may require some additional considerations and preparations such as:

- extra visual materials;
- vocabulary lists and models of sentence structures;
- recognition that EAL pupils may want to do preparatory work in their first language before making a contribution in English;
- recognition that a pupil may not want to speak at all but be happy to make a drawn or written contribution;
- particular care about the composition of the group or pair and the feelings and perceptions of its members;
- it is not a good idea to have a group where all members share a first language because EAL learners need good pupil models of English;
- it is important but sometimes difficult to avoid the situation where a partner or the rest of the group begins to resent an EAL learner because they feel that he or she is copying or needs too much support.

Case Study: Year 3

Year 3 pupil, Angela, is discussing her work with a teaching assistant. Angela has been partnered with Maria, a Filipino child who has been in the UK for about 2 months and speaks very little English. Angela asks: 'Do I have to sit with Maria again, she always copies me?' The teaching assistant explains carefully that she wants Maria to sit with Angela because her work and her speaking are good and that she is really helping Maria to learn her new language. Angela is quite pleased about this and happy to continue.

Perhaps older pupils would not be as accommodating as Angela but perhaps they also would respond to a careful explanation.

Carefully organized group work supported by sharing a first language can be very supportive, as in the case of Fulya, a Year 6 pupil who had been in the United Kingdom for six months. There were two other Turkish speakers in her class and Fulya reported that they had helped her to settle in and be comfortable in school and that she worked well with them in collaborative group work. However, Gurbet, a newly arrived Kurdish child in a different class, was not comfortable working with other Turkish speakers in her class. The other Turkish speakers were British born and mostly Turkish Cypriot and she reported that she didn't like to work with them because they didn't listen to her.

At the beginning of this chapter we said that pupils need a comfortable environment and to feel safe. With Gurbet we see an example of a pupil who did not feel comfortable and perhaps felt unwelcome in the classroom. We also see an example of a small group of pupils who share the same language but are from different cultural backgrounds which demonstrates the necessity for teachers to watch and listen to their pupils and to respond to them as individuals.

The culture of the classroom, the relationships between teacher and pupils and the teacher's approach to organizing learning are important here. Watkins (2003) refers to 'learning-centred classrooms' where all members are encouraged to see themselves as part of a community of learners rather than as a group of individual learners. A classroom such as this would be truly inclusive and would be supportive to all learners.

Communities of learners

The concept of the learning-centred classroom requires a shift of emphasis from a focus on effective teaching strategies to a focus on effective learning. In such classrooms there is more of a shared relationship between teacher and pupil, an expectation that pupils will take more responsibility for learning and a greater emphasis on building understanding through shared activity and dialogue. Central to the concept is the idea that all members of the class are encouraged to see themselves as part of a community of learners rather than as a group of individual learners. The learning environment developed through this approach to organizing teaching and learning is likely to be one which is supportive to all learners, including EAL learners.

Some of the features of the classroom as a community of learners, identified by Watkins (2001) in research conducted at the London University Institute of Education, are particularly relevant to the supportive learning environment we have been considering. The list below contains some of these features:

- Social, emotional and intellectual activities are linked.
- Dialogue between pupils is encouraged.
- Collaborative learning approaches are used.

- The environment is safe and a sense of belonging is promoted.
- Pupils have opportunities to work in small, mixed ability groups.
- Members of class show respect for each other.
- All contributions are valued.
- Everyone is included and given the opportunity to participate actively.
- Thinking time is built in.
- Pupils are grouped for performance rather than ability – no labels.
- The pupils learn from each other.
- There is flexibility.

Hart et al (2004) in *Learning Without Limits* give some interesting accounts and analyses of classroom-based, teacher-conducted research projects focusing on mixed ability teaching and collaborative learning. The *Learning Without Limits* project focuses on work done in a number of classrooms including nursery, primary and secondary, and the idea of communities of learners is central to the philosophy of learning embraced by all the teachers involved. The book of the project is built around case studies which describe and then analyse how each teacher works with the pupils in his or her class. One of the results of the analysis is a list of ten purposes for teachers which could provide a framework for developing a learning environment that supports all learners, including additional language learners.

Teachers' purposes

- Building confidence and emotional security
- Strengthening feelings of competence and control
- Increasing enjoyment and purposefulness
- Enhancing young people's identities as learners
- Increasing hope and confidence in the future
- Increasing young people's sense of acceptance and belonging
- Increasing young people's capacity to work as a learning community
- Providing successful access for all young people to whatever knowledge, skills and understanding are intended to be the focus of a lesson
- Increasing relevance, enhancing meaning
- Enhancing thinking, reasoning, explaining. (Hart et al 2004:267)

Within secondary subject teaching

In a guidance document for the Secondary National Strategy for School Improvement, the DfES set out the following key principles for the teaching of EAL pupils:

- Bilingual pupils at any level of fluency have a right of access to the National Curriculum.
- Language development arises from an oral and cognitive interplay between language and subject: de-contextualized language activities are rarely productive.
- Pupils acquire English from socializing and collaborating with peers as well as learning from explicit teaching.
- Talk and collaboration are essential elements in effective teaching and learning and in developing secure literacy skills.
- The aim of good teaching for bilingual pupils is to scaffold the learner's progress to independence. (DfES 2007:13)

Every secondary subject teacher is a teacher of language, not simply of the technical language needed for the subject but of the increasingly rich and expressive language we all need to function as members of our communities and of society. A supportive learning environment in a secondary subject class would be a language-rich environment organized by a teacher who is mindful of the importance of language in teaching and learning. Planning for the language needed to take part in activities, to understand and to demonstrate understanding in a subject area is vital for supporting EAL learners. Gibbons (1991) tells us that:

> Language is integral to most of what happens in classrooms, but to a competent language user its role is like that of a window through which we look at the content. It is transparent and although we may recognize that it is there, its transparency means that it is very hard to see. Focusing on content alone makes language the invisible curriculum in the school. And for children with poor English skills the language becomes the block to learning. To put it another way, their window is made of frosted glass. (Gibbons 1991, in Ellis 2007:156)

In 2002 the DfES, now the DCSF, produced a set of guidance materials for supporting EAL learners as part of the Key Stage 3 National Strategy and referred to in Chapter 3. The guidance was intended for heads of department and specialist language teachers but it contains advice and examples of classroom practise which are useful for all teachers. Each national curriculum subject has its own particular advisory booklet with examples from that curriculum area but the general advice is the same in each booklet, as you would expect. The booklets all have a section entitled 'A supportive learning environment' and all contain a checklist of features similar to the one from the geography document which follows.

A supportive learning environment

Schools implementing the Key Stage 3 Strategy will provide a supportive, inclusive learning environment based on the following features:

- structured lessons that draw pupils in from the start of the lesson;
- active and engaging tasks which encourage all pupils to participate;
- teaching and learning strategies that are oral and interactive;
- an emphasis on short-term planning, which includes planning for input and support from other adults in the classroom, to ensure the learning opportunities are maximized;
- subject-specific language skills and conventions of particular forms of writing, which are made explicit and demonstrated by the teacher;
- planned opportunities for oral rehearsal in pairs and in small groups;
- a requirement that pupils apply learning, supported by group work, before moving to independent activity.

(DfES 2002a:3)

It is useful to note that although the guidance documents are focused on pupils learning English as an additional language, the guidelines are expressed in terms of inclusion in general, reminding us that it is a teacher's role, or purpose as above, to provide access to learning for all our pupils. In fact the documents are all entitled *Access and Engagement* and subtitled *Teaching Pupils for Whom English is an Additional Language*.

Guidelines for welcoming new pupils

Most schools have written guidelines for welcoming pupils. A guidance document is an important part of establishing a supportive learning environment because it provides a common basis for all staff in their relations with new EAL pupils and should ensure a consistent experience for pupils. The guidelines which follow are from a primary school in central Swansea and were written with the help of the local Ethnic Minority Language and Achievement Service.

Welcoming and settling EAL pupils

The first few days

- Always place the pupil in his/her correct age equivalent year group.
- Make sure that everyone knows how to spell and pronounce the pupil's name correctly. Remember pronunciation may not be obvious from the spelling.
- Group/set the pupil with his/her intellectual peers from the outset. Remember the pupil will also need to be with strong English language peer models.
- Place the pupil with one or two sympathetic peers (if at all possible pupils who speak the same language and can translate) to help with school routines, rules and getting familiar with the geography of the building. Make sure other pupils don't overwhelm with help.
- Be sensitive to the pupil's emotional needs. He/she may be homesick, separated from other family members, or may have left a war zone. The pupil may express insecurity within the new environment in a variety of ways – passivity, aggression or even disruptive behaviour.
- A newcomer to English will rely heavily on non-verbal clues/gestures to enhance understanding. Be aware, however, that non-verbal communication can be interpreted differently e.g. a shake of the head may mean 'yes' and a nod 'no'. A pupil may have been taught not to look directly at an adult.
- For newcomers to English aim to teach very basic survival language e.g. toilet, yes, no, please, thank you, I don't understand, I've finished etc.
- Let the pupil be silent if he/she wishes. A newcomer to English may not speak English in school for several months. Don't panic – this is not uncommon.
- Expect and allow the pupil to switch off at times, learning a new language is very tiring.
- Ensure that the pupil has 'tools' for classwork/homework – pencils, books and other necessary items. Remember that the pupil may not have certain items of P.E. kit.
- Contact the Ethnic Minority Language and Achievement (EMLA) Service as soon as possible for further advice.

Swansea Primary School

Key Points

- A supportive learning environment is essential for all EAL learners.
- Information about pupils, families and culture is vital.
- Partnership teaching between teachers, TAs and specialist language support staff is important.
- Use of first language and learning by collaborating with others are important strategies to support additional language learning.
- All teachers are teachers of language as well as teachers in their curriculum areas.

Moving on: suggestions for further enquiry

- The Ethnic Minority Achievement Programme (EMAP), one of the National Strategies organized by the Department for Schools, Children and Families, publishes a newsletter which describes school-based work carried out in a variety of schools by teachers working with specialist staff. The newsletters are a valuable source of interesting and manageable strategies for all teachers and students. Have a look at some of these and pick out some ideas to try. Copies of the EMAP newsletter can be downloaded from: www.teachernet.gov.uk/publications
- Find out about your local authority Ethnic Minority Achievement service and collect any guidance materials they have produced. Many services have a website, go to the NALDIC website for links: www.naldic.org.uk/ITTSEAL2/support/LEAwebsites.cfm

Further reading

Conteh, J. (2003) *Succeeding in Diversity: Culture Language and Learning in the Primary Classroom.* Stoke on Trent: Trentham Books

Gravelle, M. (2006) *Supporting Bilingual Learners in School.* Stoke on Trent: Trentham Books

Hart, S., Dixon A., Drummond, M.J., McIntyre, D., (2004) *Learning Without Limits.* Maidenhead: Open University Press

Watkins, C. (2005) *Classrooms as Learning Communities: What's in it for Schools?* London: Routledge

Watkins, C., Carnell, E., Lodge, C.M. (2007) *Effective Learning in Classrooms.* London: Paul Chapman Educational Publishing

For more about collaborative learning and ideas for collaborative activities to include EAL learners go to the Collaborative Learning Project at http://www.collaborativelearning.org/

6 Assessment

This chapter will look at assessing EAL learners and will address the following topics:

- Initial assessment of EAL learners
- Models of levels of language development
- Summative assessment
- Assessment for learning

The topics addressed will relate to the following standards for QTS, which are the general standards for monitoring and assessment which apply to all pupils. There is a specific standard in Wales which relates to 'those learning English or Welsh where this is the language in which they are being taught and is different from the language or form of language of their home'. All pupils in Wales are either taught in Welsh or learn Welsh as another language and the interesting situation can arise where there are pupils in Welsh medium schools whose first language is English and in English medium schools whose first language is Welsh.

QTS standards for England

- Q 13 Know a range of approaches to assessment, including the importance of formative assessment.
- Q 26 (a) Make effective use of a range of assessment, monitoring and recording strategies.
  (b) Assess the learning needs of those they teach in order to set challenging learning objectives.
- Q 27 Provide timely, accurate and constructive feedback on learners' attainment, progress and areas for development.
- Q 28 Support and guide learners to reflect on their learning, identify the progress they have made and identify their emerging learning needs.

QTS standards for Wales

S3.2.1 They make appropriate use of a range of monitoring and assessment strategies to evaluate learners' progress towards planned learning objectives, and use this information to improve their own planning and teaching.

S3.2.2 They monitor and assess as they teach, giving immediate and constructive feedback to support learners as they progress. They involve learners in reflecting on, evaluating and improving their own performance.

S3.2.5 With the help of an experienced teacher, they can identify the levels of attainment of those learning English or Welsh where this is the language in which they are being taught and is different from the language or form of language of their home. They begin to analyse the language demands and learning activities in order to provide cognitive challenge as well as language support.

Initial assessment of new pupils will not be the concern of students or NQTs but is useful as background information. Summative assessment will concern all practising teachers and formative assessment, assessment for learning, is the responsibility of all practitioners: teachers, students and TAs. Assessment for diagnostic purposes i.e. the identification of additional learning needs, will not be addressed here as it needs specialist attention:

The identification and assessment of the special education needs of children whose first language is not English requires particular care. It is necessary to consider the child within the context of their home, culture and community. (SEN Code of Practice 2001 5.15)

Reflection

Think about what you know about assessment for learning. What will you need to be aware of and take into consideration when using assessment for learning with additional language learners?

Initial assessment

On entry to school EAL pupils will usually be carefully assessed as part of the school's admission procedure. This initial assessment will normally be carried out by specialist language support staff and will be conducted in the pupil's first language to try to ascertain the level of general language development. First language assessment is important because, as we have already seen, first language development is an important factor in the successful learning of an additional language. Early assessment is also important to help to distinguish between needs based on new language acquisition and other needs such as learning difficulties or speech and language difficulties. The initial assessment will enable staff to describe a pupil's competence in English according to a broad level descriptor, which is useful to give some guidance on what the pupil can be expected to do. Formative assessment will then be used to inform planning, as it is for all pupils.

There are several models used to describe, in broad terms, the stages a pupil goes through in the process of acquiring a new language and it is the descriptors of these stages which are used in the initial assessment and can be used in further summative assessments. Many local authority ethnic minority achievement services use scales of language development loosely based on the four stage model devised for the Centre for Literacy in Primary Education (CLPE) by Hester et al. (1990):

Stages of English learning: Hester et al.

The following scale describes aspects of bilingual children's development through English which teachers might find helpful. It is important to remember that children may move into English in very individual ways, and that the experience for an older child will be different from that of a young child. The scales emphasize the social aspects of learning as well as the linguistic. Obviously attitudes in the school to children and the languages they speak will influence their confidence in using both their first and additional languages.

Stage 1: new to English

Makes contact with another child in the class. Joins in activities with other children but may not speak. Uses non-verbal gestures to indicate meaning – particularly needs, likes and dislikes. Watches carefully what other children are doing and often imitates them. Listens carefully and often 'echoes' words and phrases of other children and adults. Needs opportunities for listening to the sounds, rhythms and tunes of English through songs, rhymes, stories and conversations. If young, may join in repeating refrain of a story. Beginning to label objects in the classroom, and personal things. Beginning to put words together into holistic phrases (e.g. no come here, where find it, no eating that). May be involved in classroom learning activities in the first language with children who speak the same first language. May choose to use first language only in most contexts. May be willing to write in the first language (if s/he can) and if invited to. May be reticent with unknown adults. May be very aware of negative attitudes by peer group to the first language. May choose to move into English through story and reading, rather than speaking.

Stage 2: becoming familiar with English

Growing confidence in using the English s/he is acquiring. Growing ability to move between the languages and to hold conversations in English with peer groups. Simple holistic phrases may be combines or expanded to communicate new ideas. Beginning to sort out small details (e.g. 'he' and 'she' distinction) but more interested in communicating meaning than in 'correctness'. Increasing control of the English tense system in particular contexts, such as story-telling, reporting events and activities that s/he has been involved in, and from book language. Understands more English that s/he can use. Growing vocabulary for naming objects and events and beginning to describe in more detail (e.g. colour, size, quantity) and use simple adverbs. Increasingly confident in taking part in activities with other children through English. Beginning to write simple stories, often modelled on those s/he has heard read aloud. Beginning to write simple accounts of activities s/he has been involved in but may need support from adults and other children who speak her/his first language if s/he needs to. Continuing to reply on support of friends.

Stage 3: becoming confident as a user of English

Shows great confidence in using English in most social situations. This confidence may mask the need for support in taking on other registers (e.g. in science investigation, in historical research.) Growing command of the grammatical system of English, including complex verbal meanings (relationships of time, expressing tentativeness and subtle intention with might, could etc. . . .) and more complex sentence structure. Developing an understanding of metaphor and pun. Pronunciation may be very native-speaker like, especially that of young children. Widening vocabulary from reading stories, poems and information books and from being involved in maths and science investigations and other curriculum areas. May choose to explore complex ideas (e.g. in drama/role play) in the first language with children who share the same first language.

Stage 4: a very fluent user of English in most social and learning contexts

A very experienced user of English and exceptionally fluent in many contexts. May continue to need support in understanding subtle nuances of metaphor and in Anglo-centric cultural content in poems and literature. Confident in exchanges and collaboration with English-speaking peers. Writing confidently in English with a growing competence over different genres. Continuing and new development in English drawn from own reading and books read aloud. New developments often revealed in own writing. Will move with ease between English and the first language depending on the contexts s/he finds herself in, what s/he judges appropriate, and the encouragement of the school.

The stages in this model are not age related though the descriptions in Stages 1 and 2 of this version appear to relate to very young children, as they have references to 'songs and rhymes' and 'simple stories'. An example of a similar system is the five-stage model used by the Ethnic Minority Language and Achievement Service (EMLAS) in Swansea in which the descriptions are shorter and do not have the examples which suggest age relatedness.

Ethnic minority language and achievement service Gwasanaeth cyrhaeddiad ac iaith y lleiafrifoedd ethnic

5 Stage model of English as an additional language acquisition – general descriptors

Guidance notes

Pupils make progress in acquiring English as an additional language in different ways and at different rates. Broad stages in this development are identified below as descriptions to be applied on a 'best-fit' basis in a similar manner to the National

Curriculum level descriptions. Progression from stage A to stage E can take up to 10 years and individuals are likely to show characteristics of more than one 'stage' at a time. A judgment is usually needed over which stage best describes an individual's language development, taking into account age, ability and length of time learning English.

Stage A: new to English

May use first language for learning and other purposes. May remain completely silent in the classroom. May be copying/repeating some words or phrases. May understand some everyday expressions in English but may have minimal or no literacy in English. Needs a considerable amount of EAL support.

Stage B: early acquisition

May follow day to day social communication in English and participate in learning activities with support. Beginning to use spoken English for social purposes. May understand simple instructions and can follow narrative/accounts with visual support. May have developed some skills in reading and writing. May have become familiar with some subject specific vocabulary. Still needs a significant amount of EAL support to access the curriculum.

Stage C: developing competence

May participate in learning activities with increasing independence. Able to express self orally in English, but structural inaccuracies are still apparent. Literacy will require ongoing support, particularly for understanding text and writing. May be able to follow abstract concepts and more complex written English. Requires ongoing EAL support to access the curriculum fully.

Stage D: competent

Oral English will be developing well, enabling successful engagement in activities across the curriculum. Can read and understand a wide variety of texts. Written English may lack complexity and contain occasional evidence of errors in structure. Needs some support to access subtle nuances of meaning, to refine English usage, and to develop abstract vocabulary. Needs some/occasional EAL support to access complex curriculum material and tasks.

Stage E: fluent

Can operate across the curriculum to a level of competence equivalent to that of a pupil who uses English as his/her first language. Operates without EAL support across the curriculum.

As we have said, initial assessment will be carried out by a specialist additional language teacher who will devise a plan of support tailored to the pupil's needs, in partnership with the classroom teacher. If appropriate the support of a language specialist or bilingual teaching assistant will be arranged but in the main the pupil will be supported by the classroom teacher and teaching assistant. An example of a support plan is shown here:

Extract from a support plan for a Y3 pupil

Language Development in the Curriculum		
Name: Aisha	**School: Perfect Primary**	
Year Group: 3	**Home language: Arabic**	**EAL Stage: A -**
Supported by: AB	**Academic Year: 2009–10**	
General Language Development Needs		
<ul><li>To begin to develop some social language.</li><li>To begin to express needs simply within learning and social situations.</li><li>To follow simple everyday instructions and routines.</li><li>To develop her knowledge of positional language.</li><li>To follow simple stories/oral texts when accompanied by visual aids, props etc.</li><li>To be able to tell a story to accompany pictures in a book.</li><li>To complete simple sentences using patterns with support.</li><li>To respond to text in visual form.</li></ul>		
General Strategies for Supporting Identifies Language Development Needs and Curriculum Access		
<ul><li>Pair or group Aisha with good language and role models so that she is exposed to good English and good behaviour.</li><li>Keep instructions simple and repeat them often, using gestures and facial expressions to convey meaning.</li><li>Focus on building up Aisha's basic vocabulary e.g. classroom equipment, parts of the body, actions, colours, by talking about activities she is engaged in.</li><li>Provide opportunities for Aisha to play simple collaborative activities especially barrier games, describing the position of objects.</li><li>Share books by talking about illustrations and introducing new vocabulary.</li><li>Provide sentence stems for completion e.g. I am, I like, I live in, I have etc., with visual prompts e.g. pictures of actions.</li><li>Use simple recording systems such as grids, yes/no answers.</li><li>Provide collaborative, visually supported activities such as sequencing and matching words/ sentences.</li></ul>		

Summative assessment

There are difficulties and issues involved in the testing and summative assessment of any pupil and these are made more complex if the pupil is an additional language learner. A major difficulty will be the possible disparity between the pupil's knowledge and understanding of curriculum content and the ability to express that knowledge in English, spoken or written. Many local authorities have adapted the stage models, for use in their schools, by separating the stages into speaking, listening, reading and writing, as in National Curriculum English. The scales have proved very useful and schools have used them in a number of different ways but they do not equate to the summative level descriptors for National Curriculum English. Assessment in National Curriculum English is the same for EAL pupils as it is for their first language English peers.

Other local authorities and their schools use the Extended Scale for Assessing Early Progress in English as an Additional Language, set out in *A Language in Common: Assessing English as an Additional Language* (QCA, 2000). This scale relates to listening, speaking, reading and writing, and gives two descriptions for attainment before English National Curriculum level 1 and a further two descriptions for attainment within level 1. The guidance within the document is intended to help teachers focus on particular ways of assessing pupils' early progress in English 'in such a way as to ensure that pupils' attainment is appropriately linked to their full National Curriculum entitlement.' (P5) The authors are careful to point out that the descriptors are intended as summative statements but they can also be used for formative purposes. The intention of the extended scale is to allow a common scale of attainment in National Curriculum English for all pupils:

> The common scale provides reference points for all pupils. It allows for the fact that pupils will show progress in different ways, and that the routes that they take as learners will differ. There is no expectation that for any one pupil there is only one way to fulfil the broad band of achievement described. Pupils will demonstrate different strengths appropriate to be assessed at the same level. Neither is there an expectation that pupils, from whatever linguistic starting point, will show the same profile of performance in all modes. (QCA, 2000:10)

In response to an increasing number of locally devised scales of language attainment the DfES published further guidance documents including, in 2005, *Aiming High: Guidance on the Assessment of Pupils Learning English as an Additional Language*. In this publication it is strongly recommended that schools and LEAs should not try to devise additional attainment descriptors for their EAL pupils but use only the extended scale:

> Summative assessment for bilingual pupils, as for all pupils, should be based on National Curriculum measures and, where applicable, the QCA EAL steps should

be used as an extension of the National Curriculum English scale. It is not recommended that additional, locally developed scales of fluency are used for summative purposes and LEAs should not require schools to produce performance data using locally devised fluency scales. (DfES 2005:6)

This guidance has proved controversial and according to the National Association for Language Development in the Curriculum (NALDIC) many teachers have ignored the scale, preferring to focus on general language development rather than the development of National Curriculum English. NALDIC itself has produced a number of discussion and briefing papers and in 2005 called for resources to be invested in developing a national framework for assessing English as an additional language:

Until the necessary resources are invested in developing a national EAL assessment framework, we believe that specialist staff, mainstream teachers and schools should continue to use such separate scales or measures of EAL fluency which support them in their task of enabling learners of English as an additional language to learn and achieve equitably within the education system. (NALDIC, 2005)

In January 2009 NALDIC published a trial version of formative level descriptors for KS1 and KS2 which can be found on the NALDIC website at http://www.naldic.org.uk/docs/research/documents/NALDICIntroductionto-FormativeDescriptors 300509.pdf

Formative assessment: assessment for learning

Assessment for learning is the ongoing, everyday assessment of pupils which is part of the teaching and learning cycle. The careful monitoring of pupils' learning is necessary in order to plan the next steps in taking their learning forward. Teachers gather information about their pupils by observing, listening and questioning and they use the information to intervene where appropriate and to inform their future planning.

Assessment for learning is widely accepted as a means of improving learning and raising achievement for all pupils (Clarke, 2002, 2005; Black et al., 2002, 2003) and it has been shown to have a positive influence on the motivation and self-esteem of pupils, both of which are important conditions for learning. There are several important factors involved, all of which contribute to the effectiveness of the strategy:

- Adjusting teaching to take account of results of assessment.
- The active involvement of pupils in their own learning.
- The provision of effective feedback to pupils.
- The need for pupils to be able to assess themselves and understand how to improve.

The general principles of assessment for learning are the same for all pupils but, as you would expect, with EAL learners there are additional factors to consider.

Adjusting teaching to take account of results of assessment

At the heart of assessment for learning is the use of assessment information to inform planning. Information for assessment purposes can be gathered in a number of ways while lessons are ongoing, and observing, and talking and listening to pupils are the obvious means of checking on the learning of EAL pupils. Information gathered is only useful if it is then used to plan pupils' next steps in learning and for EAL pupils this will mean development in language learning as well as in aspects of curriculum. Planning in partnership with colleagues such as other teachers, TAs and specialist language support staff is very much to be recommended, see Chapter 5.

Planned opportunities to assess

There will always be a tension between the pupil's knowledge and understanding of the curriculum content and the ability to express that knowledge in English, spoken or written. It is important therefore, especially for students and newly qualified teachers, to organize opportunities for assessment at the lesson planning stage, so that the activities planned will allow pupils to demonstrate what they know without being held back by their English language. Planning also needs to take account of the classroom management issue of giving the teacher, or the TA, the opportunity to observe or spend time with a particular pupil or group. When planning activities to provide assessment opportunities it is useful to bear in mind and make a note of the following factors because they will need to be included in the context notes in any assessment record:

- The amount of contextual support provided i.e. pictures, objects, word lists etc.
- The amount of pre-teaching.
- The language needed to understand and complete the task.
- The extent to which the activity is related to the pupil's past experience.
- The range of learning styles employed in the activity.
- The opportunity to work with a partner or in a group.
- The opportunity to work with an adult or peer who shares the same language.
- Opportunities to show initiative and demonstrate learning in a variety of ways which do not all rely upon their command of English e.g. gestures, diagrams, drawing, acting out.

(Adapted from *Hertfordshire Guidelines on Bilingual Pupils with Special Educational Needs: Assessment and Intervention*)

Assessment notes can be added to planning sheets as a running record of daily observations (see Clarke, 2001) and significant developments recorded in a weekly diary like the example in the next section.

Observation

For newly arrived pupils, particularly those with little or no English, observation is the sensible way to gather information about different aspects of progress: socially, linguistically and curriculum related. In primary schools the class-teacher can keep a running record, in the form of a diary, to record any significant developments. In fact this would simply be a more detailed version of a strategy employed by many primary teachers to record significant achievement or lack of achievement in all their pupils. A different method of regular monitoring needs to be devised in the secondary school, where pupils move from teacher to teacher, and monitoring systems will differ from school to school. The example below is a series of extracts from the diary of a year 5 teacher, recording observations of Amy, a Cantonese speaker with little English, who joined the class at the beginning of the school year. These extracts are some of the comments on Amy's social progress and show her increasing confidence with peers and adults.

Date	Observation	Date	Observation
Sept. Oct. Nov. Dec.	Arrived. Very quiet with adults and children. Reluctant to get into swimming pool in swimming lesson Anna has become her friend Took paints and sugar paper home. Very enthusiastic	Feb March April May	Asked teacher on duty to go the toilet. First time she has talked to an adult she didn't know. Asked to take home reading books in Cantonese and English Harry showed her his picture. She said 'Yours? Very nice'. Asked to read to me. More confident when swimming.

Feedback

Effective feedback, written and oral, is an integral part of assessment for learning. It encourages pupils to be actively involved in their learning and helps them to understand how they can improve. The principles are the same for all pupils:

- Feedback, mainly oral for EAL learners, should be based on clear learning intentions, shared at the outset of the task/activity. There are particular implications here for EAL pupils in ensuring that they understand the learning purpose of the task. Appropriate feedback on language, written and spoken, will also be important for EAL learners.
- Making corrections to written work without the pupil present is less effective than correcting together. Written work is best corrected through re-reading with the pupil: 'Does it sound right?' and re-drafting together, for example: 'I didn't enjoyed the food because it wasn't taste nice.' Can be discussed and redrafted to 'I didn't enjoy the food because it didn't taste nice.'
- With all pupils it is important to highlight success and where improvement could take place. It is also important to give strategies for improvement, often oral, and the opportunity to make the improvement suggested in the feedback. This obviously has time implications and needs to be built into session planning.
- If the feedback is written it should be expressed in a form the learner can understand and time should be allocated for it to be read. An EAL pupil will always benefit from an opportunity to discuss any written feedback.

Self and peer assessment

Self and peer assessment are important learning strategies because they encourage pupils to be actively involved and responsible for their own learning. EAL pupils need to be given the same opportunities to be involved as other pupils in the class and where appropriate this could involve use of their first language. Groups or pairs of pupils who share a first language can peer assess, or a bi-lingual teaching assistant, where available, can support an individual pupil to self assess.

A portfolio of work samples is an important record of a pupil's language development and it is a good practice to involve pupils in the selection of the work samples. This is also an opportunity for active involvement and self assessment. The selection of the samples and the learning demonstrated in the samples is a good focus for a teacher/pupil conference: a structured meeting between teacher and pupil.

Conferencing

Conferencing is a strategy used in primary and secondary schools as part of the self-assessment and feedback process. Regular one-to-one conferencing sessions give pupils the framework and the opportunity to reflect on their learning and to discuss their opinions and feelings about their progress. For EAL learners, as for other learners, this helps to bring a sense of responsibility for their own learning and for teachers it is a particularly useful opportunity to gain insight into the personal and social development of the pupil, as well as their linguistic and learning development. Conferencing can be carried out in a pupil's first language, if that is appropriate and possible, or in English by the class-teacher or TA, or by a specialist language support teacher.

Good practice in assessment

The DfES publication *Aiming High: Guidance on the Assessment of Pupils Learning English as an Additional Language.* DfES (2005) gives a checklist of good practice in the assessment of EAL pupils. Some of these points are given in the list below and can be used as a checklist for good practice in organizing learning activities in general, as all classroom tasks and activities can furnish opportunities for assessment for learning.

Points to consider

- Being bilingual affords children linguistic and cognitive advantages so learning English as an additional language should not be seen as a learning difficulty.
- Understanding usually precedes speaking and writing. Pupils with limited exposure to English can usually understand more than they can say.

- EAL learners follow different pathways to fluency and may demonstrate an uneven profile in the development of listening, speaking, reading and writing.
- Some older learners who have had significant educational experience and are literate in their first language may find reading and writing easier than speaking and listening.
- Listening is an active skill for pupils new to English. It forms an important first stage of the learning process. Pupils may opt to be silent while acquiring a considerable degree of understanding. It is therefore important to assess listening separately from speaking at this stage.
- Personality and preferred learning style impacts on rate of progress of (especially oral) language acquisition.

Conditions for assessment

To make the conditions of assessment as favourable as possible for bilingual learners:

- Ensure tasks are set in a familiar and meaningful context.
- Ensure tests and tasks are as far as possible free from cultural bias (while recognizing that no test can be completely culture-free) and provide additional support where necessary to remove barriers to learning.
- Ensure observations include situations where pupils can speak and listen in English in a non-threatening situation (e.g. as part of a small group activity).
- Provide opportunities for pupils to demonstrate understanding through use of their first language.
- Encourage and promote use of dictionaries in first language/English.
- Give pupils time to respond and try not to interrupt the flow of an answer.
- Don't over-simplify questions. Extend communication by using more complex language and allow pupils the opportunity to demonstrate the breadth of their knowledge.

(Adapted from DfES 2005: 22, 23)

Key Points

- Formative assessment is important for the learning of EAL pupils, as it is for all pupils.
- It is important to be aware of the range of factors affecting reliable assessment of EAL pupils.
- Partnership teaching helps in effective assessment and planning for EAL learners.

Moving on: suggestions for further enquiry

- Find out how your school monitors and assesses EAL learners. Does it make use of any LEA produced assessment scales?
- Visit the NALDIC website and see the NALDIC EAL Formative Assessment Descriptors (trial) http://www.naldic.org.uk/docs/research/documents/NALDICIntroductiontoFormativeDescriptors 300509.pdf accessed 25.3.10

Further reading

DfES (2005) *Aiming High: Guidance on the Assessment of Pupils Learning English as an Additional Language.* London: DfES

Hall, D., Griffiths, D., Haslam, L., Wilkin, Y. (2001) Assessing the Needs of Bilingual Pupils: Living in Two Languages. 2nd Edition. London: David Fulton

QCA (2000) A Language in Common: Assessing English as an Additional Language. Suffolk: QCA

General Strategies to Support EAL Acquisition

7

In this chapter we will look at some general strategies and activities which can be used to support pupils in the earlier stages of acquiring English, the first two stages of the development scales introduced in Chapter 6. The strategies and activities are organized in themes, some of which will be familiar from earlier chapters. General strategies such as these will continue to be appropriate for pupils who are developing their competence beyond the early stages, as we will see in Chapter 8.

The themes are:

- Peer support
- Use of first language
- Non-verbal communication
- Talk
- Visual and contextual support
- Use of support staff

The particular standards for QTS which relate to EAL learners are listed here but it will be apparent that working with the ideas described will also address other standards because they are based on sound principles of teaching and learning for all.

QTS standards for England

Q 18 Understand how children and young people develop and that the progress and well-being of learners are affected by a range of developmental, social, religious, ethnic, cultural and linguistic influences.

Q19 Know how to make effective personalized provision for those they teach, including those for whom English is an additional language or who have special educational needs or disabilities, and how to take practical account of diversity and promote equality and inclusion in their teaching.

QTS standards for Wales

S3.1.3 They select and prepare resources, and plan for their safe and effective organization, taking account of learners' interests and their language and cultural backgrounds, with the help of support staff where appropriate.

S3.3.5 They are able to support those learning English or Welsh where this is the language in which they are being taught and is different from the language or form of language of their home, with the help of an experienced teacher where appropriate.

Reflection

Think about your classroom and the kinds of learning activities you organize. What opportunities do you provide for pupils to work in pairs or small groups? Do you organize activities which promote speaking and listening?

Before beginning to look at support strategies it will be useful to look again at the level descriptors for the two earliest stages of language acquisition, as used by the Ethnic Minority Language and Achievement Service in Swansea. This will serve as a reminder of what can be expected of additional language learners in these early stages; however, as all pupils are individuals they are likely to show characteristics of more than one stage at the same time.

Stage A: new to English

May use first language for learning and other purposes. May remain completely silent in the classroom. May be copying/repeating some words or phrases. May understand some everyday expressions in English but may have minimal or no literacy in English. Needs a considerable amount of EAL support.

Stage B: early acquisition

May follow day to day social communication in English and participate in learning activities with support. Beginning to use spoken English for social purposes. May understand simple instructions and can follow narrative/ accounts with visual support. May have developed some skills in reading and writing. May have become familiar with some subject specific vocabulary. Still needs a significant amount of EAL support to access the curriculum.

Some of the activities and strategies described will be illustrated with examples from school practice, school-based projects and guidance materials from several Local Education Authorities.

Peer support

In general

Peer support is important to all pupils new to a school and even more so to someone who has arrived from a different country and cannot speak the language. Pupils who are new to the school and new to English will need to be welcomed and helped to feel comfortable. A simple and obvious strategy is to arrange one or two 'buddies' to help with school routines and finding the way around the school, but not so many helpers that the new pupil is overwhelmed. A pupil who shares the same first language would be ideal but where that is not possible a willing, friendly classmate would be appropriate. In the secondary school it will be important that the buddies are in the same teaching groups. Many local education authorities, through their Ethnic Minority Support Services, have set out guidelines for welcoming new EAL pupils. The following is an extract from the guidance materials from Milton Keynes Ethnic Minority Achievement Service.

Extract from Milton Keynes Ethnic Minority Achievement Service Guidance Materials (2004)

Pairing and Mentoring
Set up a 'buddy system' as soon as the pupil arrives

- Where possible with same language speaker
- Friendly and out-going pupil
- Good role model of English. Guard against placing EAL learners in groups with pupils with Special Educational Needs.
- If there is a pupil with the same first language in another class make arrangements for them to meet at other times.

In lessons

Working in pairs

Peer support in lessons, in groups or pairs, is important as it provides emotional as well as cognitive scaffolding. We saw in Chapter 5 that pairing pupils with others who speak the same language is not always straightforward, but careful pairing or grouping with supportive peers is a positive and successful strategy, especially when accompanied by targeted resources. The following very simple case study, provided by a TA, demonstrates the strategy.

Case study: Year 7 Science

This is a mixed ability class of 31 pupils with 13 additional language learners: Polish, Portuguese and Filipino. The pupils have to write up an experiment on 'energy'. Pupil B is a Polish student whose English is at the early acquisition stage and is improving rapidly. He has been given word tiles with the key words for the task in English and in Polish and is seated beside pupil A who will provide a good model of spoken English. A demonstrates to B how to complete the diagram and label it and shows him how to write up the experiment in steps. The boys are happy to work together.

A simple principle to apply throughout the curriculum and the key stages is to avoid individual worksheets. EAL learners will always benefit from the psychological support, and the language support provided by competent peers cannot be overestimated.

Working in groups

Another extract from Milton Keynes Ethnic Minority Achievement Service Guidance Materials (2004) extends the idea of supportive group work.

Collaborative Activities

Plan for regular collaboration with peers

- Group tasks facilitate involvement, belonging and the need to experiment with language in order to complete a task
- Language is modelled by peers
- If pupils have been taught how to work collaboratively the group creates a non-threatening environment for learning.

Support for EAL learners within group work can take a number of forms. An obvious one is the support of another speaker of the same language but good support can come from carefully structured group tasks complemented by appropriate visual resources and first language prompts.

The Milton Keynes Guidance above refers to pupils being '*taught how to work collaboratively*'. It is very easy to put pupils into groups and give them a task but all too often the collaboration is not there and some pupils will do the work while others look on. The jig-saw approach, below, gives a structure for group work which uses flexible groupings and requires every group member to take part. Two different groupings of pupils are used: Home groups and Expert groups, and these can be organized by the teacher according to the needs of the pupils.

The jig-saw approach to group work

Home groups

The class is divided into groups – four or six in a group is a good number – and a common task is set, for instance making an information booklet, a game or a magazine. The groups are given a set of jobs or questions related to the task, one for each group member, and the jobs are allocated through negotiation, with teacher support where necessary.

Expert groups

The pupils regroup according to the job or question they are working on. They work together on their particular task and become 'experts' in that particular area.

Return to home

The original Home groups reform, the members pool their different areas of expertise and work together to complete the original task – the game or booklet for instance.

EAL pupils can be helped, 'scaffolded' in the Expert groups, in a number of ways. In the example here a Year 6 pupil, Fulya, was working in an Expert group, finding out about the lives of children in Victorian times. Her group was working on living conditions and had a number of reference books, pictures and written sources. Each member of the group had a recording grid to make notes on their findings, including their reference source. Fulya had some prompts in Turkish on her recording sheet and extra picture sources to show houses belonging to the poor, middle class and rich.

Research – Houses

Children (Çocuklar)	Houses (Evler)		Living Conditions	Reference Book (Kitap)
	Inside	Outside		
Poor children (Fakir Çocuklar)				
Middle class children				
Rich children (Zengin Çocuklar)				

Fulya filled in her sheet partly in Turkish and partly in English. She was able to contribute to her Home group fully with the help of a fellow Turkish speaking pupil who was able to translate. As with most strategies to help EAL pupils this one involves a combination of support methods: peer support, use of first language and additional visual resources.

Use of first language

Involving home and family

- We have seen in earlier chapters that a pupil's home language needs to be developed as well as English, as continued proficiency in the home language supports academic achievement. For early learners it is helpful to focus on vocabulary for concepts that are familiar in the home language and to involve the family by sending home pictures, diagrams and word lists. The intention of this is to help to develop new vocabulary in the home language. Unless their English is fluent family members should be encouraged to speak mainly in their first language in the home for two reasons: to continue the development of the first language of their child and in order to avoid presenting a less than satisfactory model of spoken English.
- Sometimes parents or members of an ethnic minority community might come in to school to give support in the classroom. This is not likely to be something a student or newly qualified teacher would be able to organize but it is something one would have to plan for if such an additional helper were available. Good uses of such a person would be to support a discussion, in first language, about the topic being studied, or asking them to translate key vocabulary, captions for displays or labels for items in the classroom.

In the classroom

- With a new learner it is important to show that their first language is valued. Some everyday words and phrases in the first language – *please, thank you, hello* – can be learned by the teacher, TA and other pupils, and bi-lingual labels and signs can be placed around the classroom. Bi-lingual dictionaries and word lists are readily available, particularly through the local ethnic minority support service, and pupils can work together to teach each other and make appropriate signs. Activities which involve labelling can be used in most curriculum areas and pictures, diagrams and sketches can be labelled in first language, English or bilingually. Bilingual books, particularly story books, are a valuable addition to primary book corners.
- As confidence grows pupils can be encouraged to use their first language to discuss the answer to a question, if there is a classmate or bilingual teaching assistant who shares their language, and then explain the outcome to the teacher or group in English. They can also be encouraged to plan and make a draft of their work in their first language as this will help them to think through and organize the content before grappling with the language.
- Different pupils will be able to express their ideas in different ways, according to the task they are working on. For example, a Year 6 pupil who has excellent literacy skills in her first language, Turkish, chose to write up the results of her research into living conditions in Victorian England (see the recording grid above) in Turkish. Rather than trying to give a direct translation of her Turkish text, which she felt

unable to do, she decided to organize the information under headings and was able to use the descriptive writing within her present range of English skills. She chose to do this task, which was a whole class summative piece of work, unaided as she prefers not to be singled out and likes to work on activities set for the whole class. The staff monitor her progress as they do with all pupils in the class and give support where needed.

- Another way of working, frequently observed in the secondary classroom, is where a pupil produces a piece of writing in their first language and then translates it using a dictionary, with the help of a teaching assistant or bilingual teaching assistant where available.
- It may be necessary to negotiate with pupils some rules for using their first language. Although use of first language will be encouraged in the main, there may be times when only English speaking and writing is needed for example when encouraging fluency in English and when practising the language needed for writing. As always the language use will be determined by the nature of the task.

Non-verbal communication

- Early English learners rely heavily on gestures and non-verbal signals to aid their understanding, and pointing to or picking up items is an obvious way to help pupils learn the words for objects around them. However, it is important to be aware that different cultures may use some gestures in different ways and this can lead to misunderstandings. For instance a nod of the head may mean 'no' and a shake may mean 'yes'. In British culture it is usual to look at a person when they are speaking to you but in some cultures it is disrespectful for a child or young person to look directly at an adult when being spoken to, so a pupil who refuses to make eye contact with an older person may be showing respect rather than defiance.
- Some primary schools teach Makaton sign language to all their pupils so that simple communication, in the first instance, does not depend upon learning a more complex verbal language. You can find out more about Makaton from the organization website: http://www.makaton.org/

Case study

- *Rachel Williams The Guardian*, Thursday 2 October 2008

  Polyglot pupils turn to signing Buzz up!

Staff and pupils at a primary school where the children speak 26 languages have turned to sign language to ease their communication problems. Lithuanian, Polish, Arabic, Farsi, Japanese, Mandarin, Wolof and Shona are among the mother tongues of the 55 pupils at Fairlight primary school in Brighton for whom English is not their first language. Now all the school's 300 children – and their teachers – are learning to finger-spell words in British sign language and communicate their emotions and feelings using the signing system Makaton. Since the start of the new term assemblies have begun with a signed 'good morning'.

The head teacher, Damien Jordan, said the techniques helped pupils who might otherwise get frustrated they could not make themselves understood, as well as being popular with English-speaking attendees. Children who had previously been divided by a language barrier were now communicating among themselves. 'They think it's fantastic,' Jordan said. 'It makes them proud of their languages and proud to be able to communicate with each other. They say "It's great, because we're all learning at this stage so we're all at the same starting point".'

Fairlight's diversity stems from the fact it attracts many pupils whose parents are international students or academics, he added. Some children arrive at the school and nursery, which cater for 3- to 11-year-olds, already able to speak two or three languages.

Such is the popularity of the signing venture that staff are having to work hard to keep up with their pupils' enthusiasm. 'We've even got children inventing their own signs for things. They want to know practical things as well – they keep asking me "What's remote control, what's PlayStation?" '

Talk

- Talk is central to the learning of language, so it is very important that new EAL learners have opportunities to listen to good English and to speak when they are ready. As we have mentioned above we need to arrange pair and group work carefully so that that the learner can be with supportive peers who can model good English. It is not appropriate to put a new EAL learner with the less able pupils in the class who have TA support, as these pupils may not be sufficiently articulate to provide a good language model. The use of talk partners or small groups before written work is always useful as talk supports learning of concepts and helps pupils to sort out their ideas. Initially a talk partner who speaks the same first language would be desirable but this will not always be possible.
- One to one or small group work with the teacher or TA will provide opportunities for the adult to model different kinds of talk. For instance the teacher can describe exactly what he or she is doing, as a self-directed monologue, while carrying out a task. This will demonstrate to the pupil how to talk about an activity and with stress on key words will help to develop the particular vocabulary needed for the task. A similar monologue can accompany the pupil's activity but in this case the teacher or other adult will describe what the child is doing. Here the talk is particularly

meaningful because the pupil is involved in the activity and is listening to a commentary on their actions.

- Following a sequence of instructions can be difficult for many pupils, not only EAL learners. If there is a sequence of commands to follow it is best to pause between each one and encourage the pupil to repeat the instructions. Gestures can be useful to clarify instructions and taking more time to give instructions will give the pupil more time to process the information.
- When a pupil begins to speak English there are several simple ways to encourage and enhance their language:
- Repeat key words when saying a sentence or phrase, for example, '*Here is a pen. This is Michael's pen, this is Jane's pen.*'
- Restate: when pupils make a language error repeat back what they have said, in a corrected form, without drawing attention to the error. This is important in order to model and reinforce the correct form while maintaining the pupil's confidence.
- Expand the pupil's language by repeating and expanding their sentences, for example, the pupil's statement '*that big boat*' can become '*yes, that's a very big boat. It's a fishing boat*'.
- Using open-ended questions rather than looking for simple yes or no answers will stimulate thinking and promote extended vocabulary, as it does with all learners, and a useful way of modelling how to ask and answer questions is to use 'hot-seating'. A pupil role-plays a character, from a book or from history for example, and answers questions asked by other pupils. This is also another method of generally extending vocabulary.
- Circle time, used in many primary schools, gives an opportunity to listen and so to extend vocabulary, even when the pupil does not want to speak.
- Simple collaborative games, such as barrier games and Kim's Game, involving descriptions and positional language.

Developing vocabulary

A pupil new to English will be learning both the language of everyday life and the language of the curriculum and learning. Much everyday vocabulary will be learned from peers in their interactions in class, the playground and around the school but there are some basic strategies we can use to help general vocabulary development. The following suggestions are adapted from Elks and McLachlan (2008):

- Introduce a few new words at a time.
- Give the student a list of target vocabulary.
- Explain new words in simple language and check for understanding.

- Use multi-sensory learning:

  See it (use artefacts, photos etc.)
  Hear it
  Say it
  Read it
  Write it

- Focus on useful words: classroom equipment, parts of body, colours, actions.
- Reinforce words regularly, particularly specialist, technical vocabulary.

It is important not to assume that pupils understand the meanings of words and to make time to check and pre-teach (see below), where appropriate, any specialist vocabulary and 'command' words needed to carry out a task. The suggestions for developing a language-rich environment, given in Chapter 3, are relevant here.

Visual and contextual support

Pre-teaching

When supporting academic learning it is important to provide the pupil with as much contextual information as possible. Pre-teaching of key words and phrases is an important part of setting the scene for learning. Short vocabulary lists, with illustrations where appropriate, can be prepared, and the words and phrases can be translated and rehearsed before they need to be used. A TA, bilingual or not, would be useful here as would an additional adult helper. It is useful to encourage pupils, especially older ones, to keep their own vocabulary book or glossary to record any new words, in both languages where possible.

Visual resources

To help new learners to become comfortable and confident in school it is important to support them in the less academic tasks of finding their way around school and understanding class and school routines. If they are worried and anxious about what will happen next they will not be able to learn effectively. Simple visual tools such as maps with symbols or drawings, timelines and visual timetables will help a pupil to feel less dependent on others and more confident. The following case study comes from a classroom research assignment carried out by a teaching assistant.

Case study: Visual Timetable and Feelings Cards in Year 3

Andy, a Filipino pupil, had been in the UK for three months and joined the school in Year 3 where there were no other Filipino speakers. He seemed young for his age, was 'silent' and attached himself to the TA whenever he could. In consultation with the language support teacher attached to the school it was decided to give him visual supports: a visual timetable and feelings cards, to help his independence. The class teacher was reluctant initially because she thought he already understood quite a lot of classroom routines and that the idea was more suited to younger children. The TA, however, was keen to try it out and made a simple timeline for the day with photographs of the daily class routine and a chart with faces showing different feelings. The teacher and TA are both pleased with the response. Andy consults the visual timetable at the beginning and during the day and appears more confident and less dependent upon the TA. The other pupils in the class have been seen to consult it too and some have commented that they find it helpful. The TA also reports that the feelings cards seem to have eased the frustration that sometimes resulted in Andy simply 'switching off' and crying.

Pictures, photographs, objects, diagrams, flow charts and tables are all valuable resources, as are picture/word banks and vocabulary cards for key words. Sequencing, and labelling and matching activities, involving pictures or diagrams linked to words and phrases can be used across the curriculum and will allow the pupil to engage with the curriculum content at the same time as learning the language.

Pictures and artefacts in History and Geography

Pictures, photographs and artefacts are essential resources in the teaching and learning of history and geography.

- A simple but effective activity can be organized involving the questioning of picture sources using a picture in a text book, photographs from a photo pack, postcards (National Portrait Gallery and other gallery and museum sets, for example) or even magazine illustrations. Organize pupils into pairs or small groups and give each group a picture placed in the middle of a large piece of paper. The pupils write their ideas or questions about the picture onto the paper in whichever language they feel comfortable. They can then be helped, in whatever way is most appropriate, to assemble and process their ideas or answer the questions they have generated.

Other simple picture-related activities are:

- writing captions for photos
- writing comments in speech or thought bubbles for people in photos
- making lists of the different objects or features seen in the photo
- answering teacher generated questions about the photo, such as 'where do you think this is?' 'what do you think is happening?' Language prompts, as in the Victorian Housing recording grid, can be used where necessary.

For all of these activities pupils can use whichever language is most comfortable and they can be helped to translate into English, where necessary, after the process of thinking about the content. The activities can all be carried out with objects and artefacts as well as pictures, and the language generated can then be used as a starting point to produce a more sustained piece of writing.

Video

TV and videos are an important part of the home life of most pupils and they are a valuable classroom resource. Pupils often retain more information from a video than they do from a comparable written source, probably because it is more immediate and therefore easier to engage with. To make the most of a video it is useful to show it more than once, even though time is always a constraint, because learning is better if more time is allowed for engagement with the content and for processing the information. One way to do this is to show the film, complete or in sections, without asking pupils to make notes, followed by a short discussion to rehearse any key vocabulary. In the second showing pupils can be asked to take notes, either general notes, or focused on particular information. Support for all pupils, including EAL learners, can include pre-teaching of key words with easily visible word banks, and recording frames for notes, with prompts if needed. The following examples show note-taking sheets used in a Year 5 class to accompany two short videos in a geography topic about a locality in Kenya. The sheets were given to all the pupils and the two EAL learners in the class, both with two years English language experience, were able to complete the notes satisfactorily and join in the class discussion.

Example Video A: Pupils were asked to circle appropriate answers.

Video A Notes
1. What crops are grown? rice wheat potatoes corn fruit
2. What is the weather like? hot rainy cool cold dry
3. What lessons do the children have? Arabic Art History English P.E.

Example Video B: Pupils recorded what they saw in the different categories. The notes were written up later, after a class discussion, and then used as a basis for a piece of extended writing on the jobs done by men, women and children.

Video B Notes		
Animals	Forms of Transport	Jobs – at home and at work

Value and use support staff

The importance of partnership teaching and role of teaching assistants has been mentioned in earlier chapters but it can be difficult for students and new teachers to know how to use TAs effectively. The DfES (2002e) has produced a set of training materials for teaching assistants working in classrooms with EAL pupils. The materials are intended to be used for in service training but some of the basic strategies are useful here both for TAs themselves and for teachers and students who need to plan for their TAs in the classroom.

Ways in Which TAs can Support Pupils who are Learning English as an Additional Language:

Speaking and Listening

- Welcome and show a positive attitude to bilingualism.
- Engage the pupils in conversation and encourage as much spoken response from them as possible, inside and outside the classroom.
- Sit with them and act as a mediator.
- Speak to them directly and help them join in with class and group activities.
- Help them to contribute to group discussion.
- Provide models of English language use in different contexts.

Reading and Writing

- Tell stories and share books.
- Talk about stories and illustrations.
- Use taped versions of books.
- Act as a scribe occasionally to record their ideas.
- Help run reading, homework and other clubs.
- Help with the drafting and editing of written work. Written work is best corrected through re-reading – 'Does it sound right?' – and re-drafting together. DfES (2002e)

Advice from the expert practitioner

The following list of guidance pointers for students and newly qualified teachers was suggested by a specialist language support teacher, based in a large primary school.

- Make sure to greet pupils regularly, with their correctly pronounced name, and give status to their ability to communicate in more than one language.
- Consider levels of listening and attention. It is more difficult to maintain concentration in a less familiar language and some pupils may need to take 'time out'.
- 'Don't think they know nothing'. Be aware that learners will often be coming to school with several years of schooling experience in their home country. Many learners will be learning new ways of expressing knowledge they already have.

- Do not talk too much and be aware of the complexity of the language you are using – simplify sentence structure, length and vocabulary where necessary and emphasize key words with slight stress.
- Use plenty of visual materials.
- Group EAL learners with the more able pupils.
- Do not make pupils talk before they are ready – it is quite normal for EAL pupils to have a 'silent period'.
- Correct mistakes, without drawing attention, by modelling.
- Get to know the pupil's background and be sensitive to cultural needs.
- Encourage parents to speak and read with their children, in their home language. Do not ask the parents to speak English at home.

Key Points

- Remember the social and emotional aspects of learning and provide 'buddies' and paired and group work.
- Make use of a pupil's first language, for learning.
- Repeat, restate, expand.
- Plan activities with visual and practical resources, and pre-teach.
- Make good use of support staff.

Moving on: suggestions for further enquiry

- The standards for QTS at the beginning of this chapter are the particular standards relating to EAL learners. Refer to the standards for QTS in England or Wales and identify other statements relevant to the themes and topics within the chapter. The documents are available at: www.tda.gov.uk/qts; http://wales.gov.uk/legislation/subordinate/nonsi/educationwales/2009/3220099/?lang=en
- Investigate the NALDIC website for suggestions for classroom activities and resources: www.naldic.org.uk
- Other useful websites to investigate are:
- www.literacytrust.org.uk
- www.multiverse.ac.uk
- www.qca.org.uk

Further reading

Conteh, J. (ed.) (2006) *Promoting Learning for Bilingual Pupils 3–11*. London: Paul Chapman.

Walters, S. 'English as an Additional Language' Chapter 13 in Ellis, V. (ed.) (2007) *Learning and Teaching in Secondary Schools*. Exeter: Learning Matters

8 Developing Competence in English

This chapter follows on from Chapter 7 by looking at ways to support EAL learners as their English language skills develop. It also relates closely to Chapter 4, A Language Rich Environment. Topics will include:

- Planning – the Cummins Framework
- KS2/KS3 transition
- Extending vocabulary
- Extending writing

Standards for QTS will be the same as in Chapter 7 but the general standards in the sections on professional skills, teaching and monitoring assessment will also be relevant and do not need to be given here.

> ### Reflection
>
> Think about the different curriculum areas you teach – you may teach the whole curriculum in primary school or one or two subjects in KS3. What opportunities do you provide for your first language English pupils to develop and improve their reading and writing skills in different curriculum areas? Do you plan activities for speaking and listening?

Developing language competence

It will be useful here to reiterate the descriptors of the later stages of language acquisition taken from the Swansea guidance used earlier, as a reminder that language support is not finished when the pupil can communicate effectively in the playground and in everyday life. Many pupils in upper Key Stage 2 and in Key Stage 3 will be operating within Stages C and D.

Stage C: developing competence

May participate in learning activities with increasing independence. Able to express self orally in English, but structural inaccuracies are still apparent. Literacy will require ongoing support, particularly for understanding text and writing. May be able to follow abstract concepts and more complex written English. Requires ongoing EAL support to access the curriculum fully.

Stage D: competent

Oral English will be developing well, enabling successful engagement in activities across the curriculum. Can read and understand a wide variety of texts. Written English may lack complexity and contain occasional evidence of errors in structure. Needs some support to access subtle nuances of meaning, to refine English usage, and to develop abstract vocabulary. Needs some/occasional EAL support to access complex curriculum material and tasks.

Stage E: fluent

Can operate across the curriculum to a level of competence equivalent to that of a pupil who uses English as his/her first language. Operates without EAL support across the curriculum.

A framework for planning

Good planning, based on formative assessment, is one of the foundations of good teaching. In Chapter 3, the Cummins Framework was introduced in the context of language development and the two important aspects of language that pupils need to develop: Basic Interpersonal Communication Skills (BICS) and Cognitive Academic Learning Proficiency (CALP). The Framework was devised by Jim Cummins in 1984 as a framework for 'thinking about the learning needs of different groups of pupils so that they can operate more autonomously in the classroom' (Hall et al 2001:50). It is generally recognized as a useful way to think about planning which tries to ensure that new knowledge and skills are taught within a context which is meaningful to the pupil.

The Framework focuses on two aspects of a task: contextual support and cognitive demand. Contextual support means providing a meaningful context to the content of the task; using familiar objects, picture sources, real situations etc., so that the content and the related language are not a barrier to learning. Opportunities to use first language are also important here. Cognitive demands relate to two different sets of factors:

- The cognitive skills and processes required by the task. These range from simple skills such as naming, describing, sorting, matching and retelling to higher order skills such as classifying, comparing, generalizing, justifying and deducing from evidence.
- The knowledge, skills (including language), and learning preferences brought to the task by the pupil.

Both contextual support and the cognitive demands of a task can be varied according to the needs of the individual pupil so when an EAL pupil finds a task difficult it is important to consider whether the problem is caused by the context and language of the task or its cognitive complexity. This way of thinking can help in the task of differentiating appropriately for individual learners by adapting both the contextual support and the cognitive complexity of a task as the pupil's understanding of English develops. A simple introduction to the Cummins Framework is available at http://www.collaborativelearning.org/theorypaper.pdf and examples of plans written with the Framework, for Key Stage 2 and Key Stage 3, can be found in Hall et al (2001).

Transition from key stage 2 to key stage 3

The transition from primary to secondary school is often a cause for concern. For some pupils there are few problems but for many there is a drop in achievement as they come to terms with a new learning environment and different routines. For additional language learners there can be further difficulties working with a larger number of teachers who may not know them, their achievements and their needs.

An interesting project was carried out in Hampshire in 2003 in response to research following up success of the National Literacy and Numeracy strategies in primary schools in England. Data showed that success in literacy and numeracy in Year 6 was not sustained over the first two years of secondary schooling: 'some pupils been merely 'treading water', while others have actively regressed'. The local Ethnic Minority Achievement (EMA) Service organized a research project to examine some of the issues arising from the transfer of bilingual and ethnic minority pupils from Year 6 to Year 7.

The following findings are particularly relevant here:

- Occasionally information regarding a pupil's home language was not transferred to the secondary school because the pupil was not thought to have 'a problem' with English. As a consequence some children were given less than adequate recognition of their achievement in having made tremendous progress as new arrivals to Britain some years previously, with very little English at all.
- Other children had a need to continue with their EMA support, particularly at the beginning of term when they faced completely new experiences – a complex timetable, changes of room, new teaching styles from a variety of staff but although the receiving school was notified of this need, albeit verbally, there was a disappointing lack of take-up, probably due to expense or lack of conviction about the benefit to be derived.
- There were some instances of EAL pupils failing to hand in homework on time. On investigation this sometimes proved to be due to lack of understanding about the task. In one case a pupil lacked the necessary resource for historical research.

In another example, a reference to the Kitchener recruitment poster used in WWI and bearing the command *Your Country Needs You* had no meaning for a newly arrived Bengali speaker.

- There is still a tendency to regard underachievement in English for bilingual children as fairly natural and not immediately prompting any further investigation or action and there was a lack of familiarity with the simple, proven support strategies.
- On a positive note there was noticeably high self-esteem and confidence among pupils who had had their home language/culture acknowledged by their class tutor and even more so where they had had their home language celebrated in a photographic display.

The report made several recommendations:

- Ensure group setting is based on cognitive ability and not current performance in English, especially in the case of new arrivals – allow for rapid growth in English acquisition.
- Ensure EAL pupils are well supported across the curriculum.
- Circulate key information pertaining to EAL pupils among all subject teachers.
- Actively recognise pupils' heritage languages e.g. through whole school language displays, and advice on obtaining GCSEs in heritage languages.
- Ensure resources are provided for homework tasks, especially in the case of pupils who do not always comprehend or retain oral instructions.
- Provide models for tasks to enable parents or older siblings to support at home.

Adapted from *Bridging the gap between Primary and Secondary – what does it mean for our bilingual and ethnic minority pupils?* A report produced by Cameron, E. (2003) for *Hampshire Ethnic Minority Achievement (EMA) Service*.

Pupils in the upper years in primary school and who have been in Britain for several years may appear to be quite fluent in English. However, it has been observed that language development of EAL pupils often reaches a plateau in the middle primary years of school, and when they transfer to secondary school they struggle because their language skills are not sufficient to cope with the academic content required. Language use in school differs in important ways from language use outside of school and different academic subject areas have specific vocabularies, genres or registers without which the content of the subject cannot be mastered. Maths is an example of a subject area with a particular language: pupils need to learn words such as 'multiply', 'add', 'take away' in order to be able to talk about mathematical processes. Teachers of both primary and secondary pupils need to be aware of the continued support that EAL pupils need in order to develop their academic language. The DfES, in the publication *Aiming High: Guidance on the Assessment of Pupils Learning English as an Additional Language*, tells us that:

> Exposure to English alone without explicit teaching of the range of registers of spoken English and written academic language required will not usually be sufficient to ensure continued progress for bilingual learners beyond the initial stages.
>
> (DfES 2005:5)

Extending vocabulary

There is a range of non-specialist, cross-curricular words which it is often assumed are known and understood by pupils in secondary schools. These words could be called 'extended' vocabulary and include words used in instructions, sequencing, probability and other, sometimes abstract, contexts. Many of these words have several meanings, which change according to context and many pupils, not only the EAL pupils, have difficulty with them. Tables 8.1, 8.2 and 8.3, compiled by Elks and McLachlan (2008) from the National Numeracy Strategy and Key Stage 3 Strategy show some of the words which are regularly used in Key Stage 2 and Key stage 3 classrooms and have been shown to cause difficulties for a range of students.

It is important that pupils are given opportunities to use words such as those given in Tables 8.1, 8.2 and 8.3 in talk and in different contexts so that

Table 8.1 Vocabulary Used in Instructions

Primary Vocabulary		Year 7	Year 8	Year 9
Calculate	Describe	Annotate	Conclude	Contrast
Check	Discuss	Examine	Compare	Generalize
Complete	Interpret	Explore	Deduce	Survey
Construct	Predict	Investigate	Justify	
Convert	Record	Results	Prove	
Define	Represent	Solve		

Table 8.2 Vocabulary of Sequencing, Time and Exclusion

before	daily	always	sometimes	except
after	weekly	usually	seldom	apart from
later	fortnightly	often	occasionally	excluding
earlier than	monthly	frequently	rarely	Instead of
previously	annually	regularly	never	alternative

Table 8.3 Vocabulary of Probability

certain	possible	probable	impossible	unlikely
guess	estimate	risk	doubt	bias

Elks and McLachlan (2008:44)

they can develop their understanding. 'Rich scripting', see Chapter 4, is a structured approach to developing understanding, as is planned talk, using speaking frames where appropriate.

Speaking frames and connectives

Attention to connective words can support both speaking and writing. Speaking and writing frames, prompt sheets with appropriate connective words and phrases and vocabulary such as in Table 8.3, can be used to help pupils structure group discussions, individual presentations and debates and writing in different genres. Sue Palmer has produced a number of books of speaking frames, aimed at primary pupils, which will also be of use in Key Stage 3. The intention of the frames is to help pupils to move from spoken language to written language and what Palmer calls 'literate talk'. The book for Year 6 has useful sections on supporting paired, individual and group presentations and sets of connectives to frame the following language constructions, which are all important for pupils in Key Stage 3 as well as Key Stage 2:

- cause and effect
- sequence of events
- adding information
- opposing information
- generalization
- giving examples
- giving definitions
- opposing viewpoints
- summing up

The frame for 'Generalization' here gives examples of words used both in factual writing and persuasive writing when the writer wants to convey generalizations and approximations. There are also examples of 'tentative' verbs which may be used when trying to convey something which is not definite and words used in approximating time or number.

Useful words for making generalizations and approximations

Probably		Possibly	
Arguably		on the whole	
Perhaps		maybe	
Usually	generally	mostly	
May	might	could	
Tend(s) to		seem(s) to	
About	around	circa	
Approximately		roughly	

(Palmer 2004:50)

Table 8.4 Words and Phrases to use in Frames

General Phrases:	Connectives to Add Ideas:	Connectives to Compare and Contrast Ideas:
I believe . . .	Also . . .	Nevertheless . . .
I suggest that . . .	In addition . . .	On the other hand . . .
In my opinion . . .	Furthermore . . .	Another view would be . . .
My main point is . . .	Finally . . .	In contrast . . .
If . . . then . . .	In conclusion	Despite . . .
	Meanwhile . . .	

Table 8.4 gives some useful words and phrases to use when making a frame for speaking or writing but suggestions for frameworks are readily available in a range of published materials including Sue Palmer's books mentioned above.

Although there has been some concern that pupils may become over reliant on frames it has been noted by many teachers that pupils like them when they meet a new topic but tend not to use them when their confidence has grown. However, it is important that they are seen as a support and a step on the way to independent speaking and writing and not as an end in themselves.

Extending vocabulary within subject areas

Different curriculum areas require different kinds of writing which in turn require particular vocabulary and expressions. The following example shows a frame of words and phrases to support the writing of a newspaper report in history but a similar frame could be provided for tasks in other subject areas and would be helpful to many pupils, not only additional language learners. The pupils in this Year 7 class had been working on the concept of 'bias' and were asked to write a newspaper report on the Battle of Hastings:

Case Study: Extending Vocabulary in History

A Newspaper Report of the Battle of Hastings

Vocabulary for a biased report

Decide if you are a Saxon or a Norman. Use some of these words and phrases to improve your report

A Saxon Report	A Norman Report
glorious victory over Hardraada	our brave/brilliant leader
poor Harold	clever plans/strategy
Tired/exhausted	resisted the first attack
Harold's brave men	our ingenious (very clever) trick
courageous fighting	crafty cavalry
took up a strong position	slow Saxons
at a disadvantage	weak English army
even though	defenceless
in spite of	lost/wasted their advantage
hateful/sly/wicked Normans	superior tactics
foreigners	glorious victory

(DfES 2002b:12)

Extending vocabulary in talk: questioning

The basic strategies to help general vocabulary development, see Chapter 7, can continue to be used and many of the collaborative activities and approaches used to develop thinking skills, for example ranking activities and 'mysteries', encourage talk and help to extend vocabulary. Questioning is a way of encouraging all pupils to extend their thinking and their use of language and EAL pupils will learn by listening to teacher questioning and peer responses and by using what they hear as models for their own speaking. Some guidelines for teacher questioning were given in Chapter 4, in the context of developing a language-rich environment but basic ideas for improving teacher questioning include:

- Use procedural questions to extend responses and improve discussion. For example:
  - Do you agree or disagree with James?
  - Can you think of an example?
  - Can you add anything to Rhian's answer?
  - Could you give a reason for your comment?
  Is there a connection between your idea and Seraina's?

- Use questions which invite opinions and individual interpretation. For example:
  - Why do you think he did that?
  - What would happen if . . . ?
  - What do you think she will do next?
  - What would you do in that situation?

Case Study: EMAP Newsletter Autumn 2008

In an In-service session with a local specialist language teacher a group of secondary teachers considered how they could formulate better questions in order to promote more purposeful talk in their pupils. Some of the strategies they suggested were

- Give the correct answer and ask why it is correct.
- Make it an open question.
- Focus on how to work out the answer rather than going straight to it.
- Give the answer and ask what the question could be.
- Compare or contrast two statements.
- Having looked at how they could generate better questions, the teachers then considered the strategies they might employ to help pupils to give more thoughtful contributions and use a more extensive vocabulary. They came up with the following strategies:
- Reflection time: setting a specified thinking time before anyone can answer.
- Think, pair, share: think first as an individual, share thoughts with a partner, pairs join into fours to share their thoughts, or go straight into sharing with the whole class.
- No hands up rule: teacher chooses a pupil to respond after thinking time.
- Phone a friend/ask the audience.
- Six Thinking Hats – see note.
- Individual whiteboards: pupils write the answer and then show.
- Building on previous answers: ask a pupil to respond to the previous pupil's comment or answer.

Note: 'Six Thinking Hats' (De Bono 2000) is a strategy to encourage pupils to consider, and in this instance discuss, a question or issue from a number of perspectives. Each perspective has a different coloured 'hat':

- Red Hat: concerned with feelings – 'how do you feel about this?' – no need to explain or justify.
- Yellow Hat: identify and discuss strengths, positive aspects, good points.
- Black Hat: identify and discuss negative aspects, weaknesses. This hat is also for making judgements and evaluative comments.
- Green Hat: be creative and suggest new ideas.
- White Hat: concerned with facts and figures; a neutral, objective perspective.
- Blue Hat: thinking about thinking; discussing how to answer the question or how you arrived at an answer.

Supporting writing

Oral fluency in English is normally in advance of literacy development. Consequently it is important that pupils are monitored and supported beyond the early stages of English language acquisition. Even when they have a good oral competence in English most additional language pupils will need support with writing as it is generally much more demanding than reading. The general support strategies suggested in Chapter 7 can continue to be used and the use of writing frames, prompts and grids, as already suggested, can help pupils to organize and express their ideas in a structured form. Word banks and dictionaries will continue to support spelling and vocabulary which, as we have noted, will include increasingly specialized words as pupils move further up the primary school and into secondary school.

Gathering and organizing information

The ability to gather and synthesize information becomes more important as pupils progress through upper Key Stage 2 and into Key Stage 3. Strategies such as text marking are useful to help pupils identify relevant information in texts, and devices such as writing frames, grids and mind maps can help pupils to demonstrate understanding and record ideas without relying too much upon spoken and written language. Oral work in pairs and small groups, retelling information they have gathered, helps pupils to clarify their thoughts and provides different models of expressing ideas, and using a variety of texts as information sources gives different models for written work. The two examples which follow show some of these strategies in action.

Key stage 3 R.E.

This is a piece of work prepared for a Year 9 group with several pupils working within the 'developing competence' stage.

The pupils have a text about the five Ks of Sikhism. The teacher reads the text and the pupils follow. The pupils then work in pairs to mark their text, using three colours to underline the different kinds of information needed to complete the following grid:

The Amrit Ceremony		
Name of Symbol	Description	Meaning

The teacher tells the class how the Khalsa was founded and then describes the Amrit ceremony. Key words and new vocabulary are written up on the board and then pupils work in groups with cut up versions of the accounts of the Khalsa and the Amrit ceremony which they have to sort and sequence. The pupils then use their grids and sequenced accounts to produce a written account, supported by a frame of sentence starters and paragraph headings for those who need it. (adapted from DfES 2002c:19)

Women in Islam

In this example pupils text marked an information sheet containing extracts from several different sources, written in a variety of styles, about the impact of Islam on the lives of men and women. They used different colours to mark information about women and men and then discussed what they had found. The text marking and discussion formed the basis for a piece of extended writing in which they analysed different points of view on the role of women and drew their own conclusion. The writing frame below was available for any pupils who wanted to use it to organize their first draft.

Women in Islam

In Islam women were and are expected to . . . .

In addition . . . .

Moreover . . . .

Furthermore . . . .

Some people think that . . .

Others think . . . .

I think that . . .

Making notes

We have seen that grids and charts are useful ways to help pupils gather and organize information before moving on to writing and they can also be used to help with note making from videos or from pictures and written texts, as we saw in Chapter 7. The examples which follow were used with Key Stage 3 pupils in a project to support EAL pupils in Key Stage 3 humanities subjects.

The following is an extract from a note taking framework used to accompany a film about the trenches in WW1. The notes were then used to write a letter from a soldier to his family.

Life in the Trenches	
Use this grid to help you to take notes from the film. READ the questions before you watch. THINK about what you have to find out.	
Sentry Duty Why did the look-outs have to use a periscope?	*Remember: write in note form!*
Night-time activities Groups of men carried out essential activities at night. 4 of the groups were: 1. Ration party 2. Water party 3. Wiring party 4. Patrol	*Write here what each party of men did.*
Weather What does one speaker say about the effects of the weather on conditions in the trenches?	

Pupils in a Year 7 group used the following framework to make notes on a set of photos. They then chose one of the habitats described to compare, in writing, with their environment at home. You will notice the instructions and the vocabulary lists.

What Affects Where We Live?

- Look at the pictures
- Describe the pictures in words (describe means say what it looks like)
- Write in full sentences in the boxes
- Here is a list of words to help you:

snowy	mountainous
icy	sandy
high land	flat
water	very busy
buildings	people planting crops
no people	forest (lots of trees)

A Himalayan Mountains	B. Amazon Forest
C. Sahara Desert	D. Antarctica
E. Bangladesh	F. Lake District

Writing in different genres

As pupils develop their English language skills they will become increasingly able to write confidently in the range of genres they will need to succeed academically. Like their first language English peers additional language learners will need opportunities to practise writing in a variety of genres in different areas of the curriculum. They will continue to need the support of appropriate resources and talk, in pairs or groups, before written work will continue to be very important. The opportunity to share the editing of drafts before completing a task will also be beneficial.

There is a wide range of writing topics employing different genres, which can be used across the curriculum in Key Stage 2 or Key Stage 3. Those suggested below can be supported by talking, with frameworks where appropriate, and by writing frames where necessary. Other ideas are widely available in books and materials to support literacy and in curriculum related support materials.

Some suggestions for supported writing

- Report writing: newspaper article, magazine, newsletter.
- Discussion paper giving arguments for and against a proposal.
- Compare and contrast two places, poems, stories.
- Persuasive writing: presenting a point of view/argument intended to influence the reader.
- Giving instructions: a recipe, directions to a place.
- Story writing.

Example: supporting story writing

Story boards and narrative grids (see Figure 8.1) are effective ways of supporting story writing because they allow a pupil to organize the structure of a narrative before beginning to compose details. As always the pupil will need to be clear about the meanings of the different sections of the story board or grid and it will be beneficial for him or her to talk through the ideas before moving on to writing the piece.

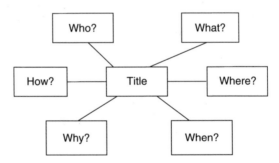

Figure 8.1 Narrative Grid

1. Narrative Grid/Spider diagram: write the title in the middle and encourage the pupil to discuss the story, with the teacher or with a partner, using the questions as prompts.

2. Story board: presented as a grid and the pupils can draw or write in each box.

Title		
Characters	Location	Start
Build up	Climax	End

This grid is also useful to analyse the plot of a book or to organize an account of a historical event. (Adapted from Elks and McLachlan, 2008b)

Example: writing in Science

In *Access and Engagement in Science*, referred to earlier, we are told that 'on average pupils spend about a third of their time writing in science'. The different types of writing are then listed with their possible purposes, showing what a wide range of genres pupils need to be able manage.

Types of Writing in Science	Possible Purposes
Answers to questions	To check understanding
Plan for an enquiry	Learn how to make decisions about how to collect evidence which is valid and reliable To learn how to set out a procedure To assess planning skills
Record of observations and evidence	To learn how to assemble evidence in such a way that it can be interpreted readily To assess recording skills
Conclusion to an experiment	To learn how to analyse evidence, construct arguments and develop reasoning skills
Evaluation of an enquiry	To learn how to evaluate procedures To check procedural understanding e.g. the need for the reliability and precision of measurements
Note taking	As an aid for revision and to help synthesize ideas To organize thinking To clarify ideas in order to write more precisely sometime later
Explanation	Help pupils make links between ideas and apply their understanding To probe understanding and reveal misconceptions, help pupils explain their thinking and ensure they distinguish between the 'how' explanations (describing how something works or how something happens) and the 'why' explanations (giving scientific reasons why something happens)
Argument	To analyse and present conflicting views To develop the skills of considering evidence To engage pupils To allow pupils to demonstrate achievement To capture creative thought
Writing up enquiries	To show how scientists report findings To assess pupil's application of key scientific ideas
Recording information	To assess understanding To summarize key points

(DfES 2002d:14)

All of these types of writing can be supported by talk and by models or frames, as above, so that pupils are clear about the structure and characteristics of the piece of writing required. As with all pupils it is important that EAL learners understand the purpose of the writing and that they have opportunities to write for a variety of audiences.

Some general principles

In 2001 Ofsted produced a report entitled *Managing Support for the Attainment of Pupils from Ethnic Minority Groups*, in which they identified features which contributed successfully to the support of EAL pupils. These features would serve as a useful checklist of the general principles and strategies outlined in this chapter, and in Chapter 7.

- Joint planning between mainstream and specialist language support staff.
- Focus on the content of the lesson, ensuring appropriate cognitive challenge.
- A parallel focus on the language necessary to complete the task.
- Activities that enable pupils to rehearse and explore the language they need.
- Opportunities to use and build on their first-language skills, where appropriate.
- Continuing support with writing through, for example, the use of matrices for organizing information and writing frames for more extended contributions.

(Ofsted 2001)

Building on this general advice the DfES booklets referred to earlier (DfES 2002a, c, d etc.) also provide checklists for providing an inclusive learning environment, which give slightly more detail on aspects of classroom practise. As always, though written for Key Stage 3 the list of features can be transferred to Key Stage 2.

A supportive learning environment

Schools implementing the Key Stage 3 Strategy will provide a supportive, inclusive learning environment based on the following features:

- structured lessons that draw pupils in from the start of the lesson;
- active and engaging tasks which encourage all pupils to participate;
- teaching and learning strategies which are oral and interactive;
- an emphasis on short-term planning, which includes planning for input and support from other adults in the classroom, to ensure the learning opportunities are maximised;

- subject specific language skills and conventions of particular forms of writing, which are made explicit and demonstrated by the teacher;
- planned opportunities for oral rehearsal in pairs and small groups;
- a requirement that pupils apply learning, supported by group work, before moving to independent activity.

(DfES 2002b:3)

Key Points

- It is important to continue to support EAL pupils beyond the early stages of additional language acquisition.
- Talk continues to be an essential support for writing.
- The use of frames and grids helps pupils to organize their thinking as well as their writing but they should always be seen as a stage on the way to unsupported writing.

Moving on: suggestions for further enquiry

- If you did not check this out for chapter 4 find the Key stage 3 guidance booklet for your curriculum area. http://nationalstrategies.standards.dcsf.gov.uk/search/inclusion/results/nav:50106
- Look again at the Collaborative Learning Project Website. Identify activities appropriate for developing competence. http://www.collaborativelearning.org/
- Investigate other websites for ideas for collaborative activities to support your EAL learners. You may need to adapt them or they may be useable as they are. Try:

www.globaldimension.org.uk
www. multiverse.ac.uk
www. naldic.org.uk
www.unicef.org.uk/tz

Further reading

Conteh, J. (ed.) *Promoting Learning for Bilingual Pupils 3–11*. London: Sage Publications

De Bono, E. (2000) *Six Thinking Hats*. London: Penguin

Palmer, S. (2004) *Speaking Frames: Year 6*. London: David Fulton

Palmer, S. (2010) *Speaking Frames: How to Teach Talk for Writing: Ages 10–14*. London: Routledge

Wragg, E.C. and Brown, G. (2001) *Questioning in the Primary School*. London: RoutledgeFalmer

Wragg, E.C. and Brown, G. (2001) *Questioning in the Secondary School*. London: RoutledgeFalmer

And try this: 'There's a kid in my class who doesn't speak a word of English!'

Minority Ethnic Language & Achievement Service

Forest Lodge Education Centre, Charnor Road, Leicester LE3 6LH

Tel: 0116 222 2606 E-mail: multi-ed@leicester.gov.uk

http://schools.leicester.gov.uk/mce

End Note 9

Inclusive practice

It will be evident from most chapters in this book that although special consideration needs to be given to additional language learners, 'Good practice for bilingual learners is good practice for all learners'. Conteh and Brock (2006:1)

Every Child Matters and *Children and Young People: Rights to Action*, referred to in the early chapters, contain outcomes and aims which apply to every child and young person in England and Wales. The United Nations Convention on the Rights of the Child sets out the fundamental rights of every child and young person on the planet. All of our pupils have the right to learn in an environment which supports them and allows them to fulfill their potential, which means that teachers much strive to find ways of reconciling the learning needs of their first language English pupils with those who are learning English as an additional language. This can be quite daunting unless the benefits brought by speakers of other languages are recognized and acknowledged, as well as the difficulties they may bring.

The principles of inclusive practice developed for mixed ability teaching in multi-ethnic classrooms give a good basis for supporting the learning of all pupils, first language English and additional language learners.

- The use of variety of strategies to take into account varied styles of learning.
- The use of thoughtfully chosen resources which reflect diversity in society and are tailored to the needs of individual pupils where necessary.
- Children's own experience, including their language, is valued and built on.
- Children are enabled to develop autonomy and responsibility for their own learning.
- Ideas and assumptions are challenged, particularly racial and linguistic stereotyping, and there is a recognition that additional language needs are not the same as special educational needs.
- Teaching and learning strategies involve collaboration rather than competition.
- Language, spoken as well as written, is seen as central to learning.

The following checklist will serve as a reminder of strategies which have been used successfully to help EAL pupils to learn English and to achieve well in our schools.

A checklist of basic strategies to support the additional language learner

1. Allow the learner(s) to plan and discuss work in their home language and then explain outcome to teacher or class in English – pair/group with other speakers of the same language if possible.
   Why? Home language needs to be developed as well as English. Continued proficiency in the home language supports academic achievement.
2. Encourage pupils to help each other.
   Why? Peer support, scaffolding: cognitive and emotional.
3. Help the learner to succeed in both academic and less academic tasks – use visual tools to help the learner understand class routine: directions in class and around school; visual timetable; timelines.
   Why? Improve self confidence, autonomy and self esteem.
4. Pair/group EAL learners with supportive and articulate English speakers.
   Why? Provide good language model.
5. If there is a sequence of commands to follow pause between each one and encourage the pupil to repeat instructions. Clarify instructions with gestures.
   Why? Allows time to process information.
6. With a new learner focus on vocabulary for concepts that are familiar in home language. Encourage the family to reinforce concepts by sending home pictures, diagrams, word lists, vocabulary maps etc.
   Why? Helps to develop new vocabulary in the home language.

7. Talk partners/groups before written work.
   Why? Children learn language by chatting with peers. Talk supports learning of concepts as well as the learning of language.
8. Use visual strategies to support vocabulary learning. Encourage pupils to demonstrate knowledge non-verbally by drawing, acting out, gesturing, demonstrating.
   Why? Encourage general communication.
9. **Expand** pupil's language: repeat and expand sentences e.g. 'that big cake' to 'yes, that's a lovely big cake. It's a chocolate cake.'
10. **Repeat** key words when saying a sentence/phrase e.g. 'here is a pen. This is Michael's pen, this is Jane's pen.'
11. **Restate**: when pupils make a language error repeat back what they have said, in a corrected form, without drawing attention to the error.
    Why? Model and reinforce the correct form while maintaining the child's confidence.
12. Use open-ended questions.
    Why? Stimulate thinking and promote extended vocabulary.
13. Self Talk: self-directed monologue. Describe what you are doing as you are doing it.
    Why? Demonstrates how to communicate about an activity.
14. Parallel Talk: describe what the pupil is doing.
    Why? The talk is meaningful because the pupil is involved in the activity.
15. Greet pupils regularly and give status to the ability to communicate in 2 languages.
    Why? Self-esteem
16. Value and use support staff.
    Why? You and the pupils need them!
17. Consider levels of listening and attention; look out for signs of fatigue.
    Why? It is more difficult to maintain concentration in a less familiar language.
18. Consider culture: looking at the speaker may not be considered respectful in the learner's home culture
    Why? It is easy to misinterpret behaviour.
19. Be aware that the learner might understand the underlying concept, if within own experience, but will have to learn the 'labels' in the new language.
    Why? Pupils arrive with prior learning and school experience and we must acknowledge this.
20. Be aware of the complexity of the language you are using; simplify sentence structure, length and vocabulary where necessary. Emphasize key words with slight stress.
    Why? When a student is anxious or upset the level of understanding will be impaired. Be aware of this and modify language accordingly. This is a likely

response with new pupils but also with older pupils if working with a new topic or a different teacher.

21. An easy acronym from Thompson (2003:76)

S	Simple, short sentences
P	pause between points or pieces of information
E	enunciate clearly
E	enthusiasm when communicating – use gestures and visual clues
CH	check for comprehension

Useful Activities

The following activities and suggestions will support the language development of all pupils and can be used across the curriculum:

Collaborative activities

Think, pair share

Pupils think about, write or decide something on their own. They share their thoughts with a partner, then form groups of four or six. A simple recording frame could be used to record initial thoughts then further thoughts after talk.

Brainstorming and concept mapping

Everyone contributes to the making of a list or general collection of words related to a topic. All contributions are accepted and any misconceptions or inappropriate words are sorted out in later discussion. The brainstorm can be developed into a more complex concept map thereby extending thinking and vocabulary, and can be used for further activities such as generating questions for further research, using a KWL grid, or for ranking or sequencing activities.

Listening to writing

The teacher reads a short text slowly and pupils listen. The teacher then reads the text again and pupils listen and make notes of key words and phrases. Pupils work with a partner to compare their notes and add to them, and then work in fours to share their notes and try to reconstitute the teacher's text.

Handling objects

- Labels, statements, phrases can be provided for a set of objects and pupils work together to match the objects with the word cards.
- Pupils work in pairs moving round a collection of objects set out around the classroom. At each object they think of a question and write it on a sheet beside the object. They also try to answer any questions asked by previous pairs of pupils. A recording sheet with boxes for questions and answers is useful.
- Pupils working together rank a set of objects according to given criteria or sequence them.

Using pictures

- Pupils work in groups with sets of photos and a set of questions written by the teacher. Pupils choose who will scribe for the group and each group member is given the opportunity to speak during the class feedback.
- Pin pictures or photos to the wall. Pupils work in pairs to write a positive and a negative caption on separate pieces of paper for each picture. When all the pairs are ready the captions are attached to the pictures. The following discussion can be related to bias in the media and different interpretations of the same scene.
- A collection of greetings cards, birthday, baby congratulations etc., makes a useful source for group sorting activities leading to discussions of stereotyping.
- Cut outs of speech or thought bubbles are useful to encourage short pieces of writing related to a picture e.g. what one or more character are saying or thinking.

Ranking and categorizing

The aim of ranking and categorizing activities is the opportunity afforded for thinking and discussion rather than getting the 'right answer'. It is important to emphasize that there is no right way to order the objects or statements and to follow up the activity with a class discussion comparing the similarities and differences between the groups.

- Pupils work in groups with a set of objects or statements on cards. They rank them according to criteria such as age, relevance and importance.
- Diamond ranking is a variation upon simple ranking. Groups of pupils are given more than nine statement cards which they have to rank in terms of relevance or importance. First they need to discard the statements they feel are least important until nine cards remain. They then rank the nine remaining statements in a diamond formation:

Diamond Ranking

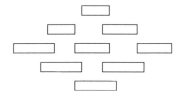

Venn diagrams, using hoops or drawn out on large pieces of paper, allow pupils to categorize objects or statements according to characteristics and to make use of the important 'shared' category.

Text related activities (DARTS)

- Text marking: pupils use coloured pens, or different kinds of underlining, to mark out particular categories of information in a text. They can then present the information in another form, for example a piece of text about a historical incident can be text marked for time/date references, people and actions and then represented as an annotated timeline.
- Pupils sequence a text which has been cut and mixed up
- Pupils classify sections of text according to categories set by the teacher.
- Pupils complete the labelling of a diagram, using other diagrams and texts for information.
- Pupils construct flow diagrams and concept maps using texts and other diagrams for information.
- 'Odd one out' activities. Pupils are given cards with statements and short pieces of text and are asked to put them into categories, under headings, and decide which is the odd one out and why.
- Matching causes and effects.

- Using true and false statements related to a text
- Grouping information to identify similarities and differences between key words and phrases.

Barrier games

General rules for barrier games are that the 'teacher' sits on one side of a barrier, a board or a big book, with a set of objects and gives information to the 'listener' who sits on the other side, with an identical set of objects. The 'listener' acts on the 'teacher's' instructions and the objective is to end up with identical results when the barrier is removed. Games can be played in pairs or with one 'teacher' and several 'listeners'.

- Use everyday objects and put them in different positions: e.g. book on the pencil; cup under the plate.
- The 'teacher' gives instruction for drawing a picture: draw a yellow circle with red dot inside, put a blue square beside the circle.
- Using model-making materials e.g. Lego, pupils take it in turns to make a pattern or model and to give instructions to the others. (from Elks and McLachlan, 2008a:54)

References

Alexander, R. (2005) *Towards Dialogic Teaching; Rethinking Classroom Talk*. UK: Dialogos

Black, P., Harrison, C., Lee, C., Marshall, B., Wiliam, D. (2002) *Working Inside the Black Box: Assessment for Learning in the Classroom*. London: School of Education, King's College

Black, P., Harrison, C., Lee, C., Marshall, B., Wiliam, D. (2003) *Assessment for Learning: Putting it into Practice*. Maidenhead: Oxford University Press

Clarke, S. (2001) *Unlocking Formative Assessment*. London: Hodder & Stoughton

Clarke, S. (2005) *Formative Assessment in Action: Weaving the Elements Together*. London: Hodder Education

Conteh, J. (ed.) (2006) *Promoting Learning for Bilingual Pupils 3–11*. London: Sage Publications

Conteh, J. and Begum, S. (2006) Using a Bilingual Approach to Promote Learning: Ideas for Talking and Writing. In Conteh, J. (ed.) (2006) 63–74

Conteh, J. and Brock (2006) Introduction: Principles and Practices for Teaching Bilingual Learners. In Conteh, J. (ed.) 2006 1–12

Cummins, J. (1984) *Bilingualism and Special Education: Issues in Assessment and Pedagogy*. Clevedon: Multilingual Matters Ltd

DCELLS (2008) Personal and Social Education Framework for 7–19 Year Olds in Wales, Cardiff: Welsh Assembly Government

DCSF: *Pupil Characteristics and Class Sizes in Maintained Schools in England: January 2008 (Provisional)*. Online: http://www.dcsf.gov.uk/rsgateway/DB/SFR/s000786/ accessed 28.11.09

DCSF (2007) *Safe to Learn: Embedding Anti-Bullying Work in Schools*. London: DCSF. Online: http://www.teachernet.gov.uk/wholeschool/behaviour/tacklingbullying/safetolearn/ accessed 11.11.09

DeBono, E. (2000) *Six Thinking Hats*. London: Penguin.

DfES (2002e) *English as an Additional Language: Induction Training Materials for Teaching Assistants in Primary and Secondary Schools*. London: DfES

DfES (2002a) *Access and Engagement in Geography. Teaching Pupils for Whom English is an Additional Language*. London: DfES

DfES (2002c) *Access and Engagement in RE. Teaching Pupils for Whom English is an Additional Language*. London: DfES

DfES (2002d) *Access and Engagement in Science. Teaching Pupils for Whom English is an Additional Language*. London: DfES

DfES (2002b) *Access and Engagement in History. Teaching Pupils for Whom English is an Additional Language*. London: DfES

DfES (2003) *Key Stage 3 National Strategy.* London: DfES

DfES (2004b) *Every Child Matters: Change for Children in Schools.* London: DfES

DfES (2004a) *Aiming High: Understanding the Educational Needs of Minority Ethnic Pupils in Mainly White Schools.* London: DfES.

DfES (2005) *Aiming High: Guidance on the Assessment of Pupils Learning English as an Additional Language.* London: DfES

DfES (2007) *Secondary National Strategy for School Improvement. Ensuring the Attainment of Pupils Learning English as an Additional Language. A Management Guide.* London: DfES

Education Reform Act 1988 (c.1), London: HMSO. Online: http://www.opsi.gov.uk/Acts/acts1988/ukpga_19880040_en_1 accessed 15.3.10

Elks, l., and McLachlan, H. (2008a) *Language Builders.* St. Mabyn: Elklan

Elks, l., and McLachlan, H. (2008b) *Secondary Language Builders.* St. Mabyn: Elklan

Ellis, V. (ed.) (2007) *Learning and Teaching in Secondary Schools.* 3rd Edition. Exeter: Learning Matters

Ethnic Minority Achievement Programme, Issue 3, Autumn 2008. Online: www.standards.dcsf.gov. accessed 20/7/09

Fellowes, A. (2006) Using Drama to Promote Learning. In Conteh et al. (2006) 75–86

Ferris, A., Catling, P., and Scott, I. (2002) *Assessing English as an Additional Language.* London: London Borough of Tower Hamlets

Franson, C. (2009) *Bi-lingual Language Acquisition.* Online: http://www.naldic.org.uk/ITTSEAL2/teaching/SLA.cfm accessed 20.3.10

Frith, U. (1989) *Autism: Explaining the Enigma.* Oxford: Blackwell

Gibbons, P. (1993) *Learning to Learn in a Second Language.* Portsmouth: Heinemann. In Ellis (ed.) 2007

Gonzales-Mena, J. (1998) *Foundations: Early Childhood Education in a Diverse Society.* Mountain View, California, CA: Mayfield Publishing

Hall, D., Griffiths, D., Haslam, L., Wilkin, Y. (2001) *Assessing the Needs of Bilingual Pupils: Living in Two Languages.* 2nd Edition. London: David Fulton.

Harrison, D. (2008) *Regardless of Frontiers. Children's Rights and Global Learning.* Stoke on Trent: Trentham Books

Hart, S., Dixon A., Drummond, M. J. , McIntyre, D., (2004) *Learning Without Limits.* Maidenhead: Open University Press

Hester, H. (1990) The Stages of English. In *Patterns of Learning.* London: CLPE. Online: http://www.naldic.org.uk/ITTSEAL2/teaching/Assessmentinschools.cfm accessed 20.01.10

Kenner, C. (2004) *Becoming Biliterate: Young Children Learning Different Writing Systems.* Stoke on Tent: Trentham Books

Leung, C. (2001) *English as an Additional Language. Language and Literacy Development.* Royston: UKRA

Milton Keynes Ethnic Minority Achievement Service (2004) *Guidance on the Assessment of EAL Pupils Who May Have Special Educational Needs.* Milton Keynes: Milton Keynes Council

NALDIC (2005) *Briefing Paper: Guidance on the Assessment of Pupils Learning English as an Additional Language.* Online: http://www.naldic.org.uk/docs/resources/documents/BriefingonAssessment.pdf. *accessed 25.01.10*

NAW (2003) *Respecting Others: Anti-Bullying Guidance.* Circular 23/2003.Cardiff: NAW. Online: http://new.wales.gov.uk/topics/educationandskills/policy_strategy_and_planning/schools/ accessed 11.11.09

Palmer, S. (2004) *Speaking Frames: Year 6.* London: David Fulton

Palmer, S. (2010) Speaking Frames: How to Teach Talk for Writing: Ages 10–14. London: Routledge

QCA (2000) *Language in Common: Assessing English as an Additional Language.* London: QCA

Ripley, K., Barrett, J., Fleming, P., (2001) *Inclusion for Children with Speech and Language Impairments.* London: David Fulton

Ofsted (2001) *Managing Support for the Attainment of Pupils from Ethnic Minority Groups.* Ofsted.: Online: http://www.ofsted.gov.uk/Ofsted-home/Publications-and-research/ accessed 6.4.10

SCAA (1996) *Teaching and Learning English as an Additional Language: New Perspectives.* London: SCAA

Sheridan, M. D. (1997) *From Birth to Five Years.* London: Routledge

Siraj-Blatchford, I. (1994) *The Early Years: Laying the Foundations for Racial Equality.* Stoke on Trent: Trentham Books

Siraj-Blatchford, I., and Clarke, P. (2000) *Supporting Identity, Diversity and Language in the Early Years.* Buckingham: Open University Press

Snow, C. (1992) Perspectives on Second-Language Development: Implications for Bilingual Education. *Educational Researcher,* 21: 16–19

Thompson, G. (2003) *Supporting Communication Disorders, A Handbook for Teachers and Teaching Assistants.* London: David Fulton

Welsh Assembly Government (2004) *Children and Young People: Rights to Action.* Cardiff: WAG

Walters, S. (2007) English as an Additional Language. In Ellis, V. (ed.) (2007)

Watkins, C. (2003) *Learning: a Sense-maker's Guide.* London: ATL

Wells, G. and Chang-Wells, G. L. (1992) *Constructing Knowledge Together: Classrooms as Centres of Inquiry and Literacy.* Portsmouth, NH: Heinemann

Wragg, E. C. and Brown, G. (2001) *Questioning in the Primary School.* London: RoutledgeFalmer

Wragg, E. C. and Brown, G. (2001) *Questioning in the Secondary School.* London: RoutledgeFalmer

Index